A Time to Heal

50 Prayer Services for the Sick and Homebound

Arranged According to the Church Year and
Including Special Prayers for Use by
Lay Ministers and Other Caregivers

John McQuiggan

Liguori

LIGUORI, MISSOURI

Imprimi Potest: Richard Thibodeau, C.Ss.R. • Provincial, Denver Province •
The Redemptorists

Published by Liguori Publications • Liguori, Missouri
www.liguori.org
www.catholicbooksonline.com

Library of Congress Cataloging-in-Publication Data

A time to heal : 50 prayer services for the sick and homebound : arranged according to the church year and including special prayers for use by lay ministers and other
caregivers / [compiled by] John McQuiggan.—Rev. and expanded ed.
  p. cm.
Includes index.
ISBN 0-7648-0930-X
1. Catholic Church—Liturgy—Texts. 2. Lord's Supper (Liturgy)—Texts. 3. Viaticum—Liturgy—Texts. 4. Pastoral medicine—Catholic Church. 5. Church work with
the sick—Catholic Church. 6. Lord's Supper—Lay administration—Catholic Church.
I. McQuiggan, John.

BX2035.6 .A5523 2003
264'.0274—dc21   2002034003

Printed in the United States of America
07 06 05 04 03 5 4 3 2 1
Revised edition 2003

If any of you is ill, he should send for the elders of the Church, and they must anoint him with oil in the name of the Lord and pray over him. The prayer of faith will save the sick man and the Lord will raise him up again; and if he has committed any sins, he will be forgiven.

JAMES 5:14–15

Contents

Foreword • xi

Author's Appreciation • xv

Introduction • xvii

Notes for Visiting the Sick and Homebound • xix

Prayer Services • 1

    Advent Week 1 • 3

    Advent Week 2 • 8

    Advent Week 3 • 13

    Advent Week 4 • 18

    Christmas Day • 23

    Holy Family • 28

    Solemnity of Mary, Mother of God • 33

    Epiphany • 38

    Baptism of Our Lord • 43

    Week of Prayer for Christian Unity • 48

    Presentation of Our Lord • 53

    World Day of the Sick • 59

    Saint Joseph • 64

    Annunciation of the Lord • 70

Ash Wednesday • 76

Lent Week 1 • 81

Lent Week 2 • 86

Lent Week 3 • 91

Lent Week 4 • 96

Lent Week 5 • 101

Passion Sunday or Palm Sunday • 107

Easter Sunday • 113

Easter Week 2 • 119

Easter Week 3 • 124

Easter Week 4 • 129

Easter Week 5 • 134

Easter Week 6 • 139

Easter Week 7 • 144

Ascension of Our Lord • 149

Pentecost • 154

Holy Trinity • 159

The Body and Blood of Christ • 164

Birth of John the Baptist • 169

Saints Peter and Paul • 174

Transfiguration of the Lord • 179

Assumption of the Blessed Virgin Mary • 185

Triumph of the Cross • 191

Saint Francis of Assisi • 196

World Mission Sunday • 201

Christ the King • 207

All Saints • 213

All Souls • 218

Ordinary Time No. 1 • 223

Ordinary Time No. 2 • 229

Ordinary Time No. 3 • 235

Ordinary Time No. 4 • 240

Ordinary Time No. 5 • 245

Ordinary Time No. 6 • 250

Service for the Seriously Ill • 255

Service for the Disabled • 260

Appendix

Communion of the Sick Outside of Mass • 267

Introduction • 268

* Communion of the Sick in Ordinary
    Circumstances • 272

    Introductory Rites • 272

    Liturgy of the Word • 275

    Liturgy of Holy Communion • 278

    Concluding Rite • 281

* Communion in a Hospital or Institution • 283

    Introductory Rites • 283

    Liturgy of Holy Communion • 284

    Concluding Rite • 286

Movable Dates for Observances of the
    Church Year • 288

Index to Prayers • 291

Sources and Permissions • 295

Foreword

Following the successful publication of a series of services designed for ministers to the sick and homebound in the United Kingdom, Liguori Publications invited its author John McQuiggan to expand the number and scope of the prayers it contained.

The result is this book, also entitled *A Time to Heal*, of more than fifty prayer services, arranged according to the liturgical year and incorporating ecumenical prayers and Bible readings appropriate for the sick and the dying. This book forms an excellent resource for visitors of the sick, residents and staff of assisted-living, long-term care, and nursing homes. This volume features an index of the subjects covered by these prayers, a calendar of movable observances that will provide users with the most appropriate service for any chosen week up to the year 2012, and the official rite of Communion for the Sick, which may be used under appropriate circumstances.

The focus of this book on ministry to the sick and homebound is a result of worldwide growth during the past few decades of the number of Christian faithful who are retired and infirm, and consequently unable to attend services in any church. The advancement of medical science in the latter part of the twentieth century has caused many terminal illnesses to become more prolonged, thus increasing appreciably the numbers of housebound people.

The compiler's experience of visiting weekly the same housebound or terminally ill people over a long period led to an appreciation for the need to develop a supply of refreshing prayers designed to keep up the spiritual interest of the sick and the infirm, and incidentally that of their visitors. Many housebound people want to retain contact with the feasts and seasons of the Church calendar. The services in this book are designed, wherever possible, to meet those needs, in reflecting on the Word, and in leading the sick person in prayer.

Those denied the privilege of attending a weekly church service look to their visiting representatives of their church for spiritual help. These sick and suffering, sometimes beyond the reach of medical recovery, who because of the nature of their illness (or injury through accident) are less able, and in too many cases no longer able, to find spiritual sustenance without direct help. They turn to God for comfort and for communication, and this can often only be provided through the medium of a visitor able and willing to read to, and pray with, them.

There are large numbers of sick people in our society today; they are tucked away from the mainstream and calling out to the only one who can really help them—to the one and only God.

One of the riches of the Christian life is the combination of the New and the Old Testaments and the Psalms, with their myriad messages of wisdom, comfort, and advice to meet most situations.

Over the years, the compiler has endeavored to gear these messages to the needs of a group of people who are spending their last years (in many cases, last ten to fifteen years) in the same home, each of them suffering from the advanced stages of illness or infirmity. This approach has proven popular with virtually all sick people visited over the years, including those fortunate enough to be in their own homes.

The author's experience of visiting the sick over many years revealed a surprising number of sick people of different Christian persuasions, eager to join in these services in nursing homes, and anxious to listen to and participate in the prayers. They seem to derive spiritual comfort from these prayer services, perhaps because they see themselves as members of a single community in one particular home, but also because they see a need in their distress to draw closer to God. These unfortunate people miss greatly their contacts with the world outside of the home, and especially their own worship community.

Such groups of people, even though severely disabled, and many of them totally dependent on others for all their physical needs, are often mentally alert and anxious to be treated as such. The type of service adopted in this book is consequently designed to vary each week for this reason.

Each service in *A Time to Heal* contains ecumenical prayers and readings culled from various sources, and adapted or written to the requirements of a service for the sick. Each service is complete and self-contained. The structure of the services provides also for specialized themes such as thanksgiving, hope, blindness, "pre-surgery," and so on. The services for the weeks of Lent are related to different Stations of the Cross, and there is a separate service for the World Day of the Sick.

This unique approach has proved to be a popular formula. The opportunity it affords to spread the Gospel has been met in the careful choice of readings. It is impossible to include all feasts, but in order to provide more flexibility, a number of services relevant to Ordinary Time has been included.

The overall purpose of this approach is to improve the relationship of the sick person to God, and to draw on the infinite supply of love and comfort that is always available from him to anyone willing to receive it; and also to refresh the sick person's spirit at a time when the body is waning.

Author's Appreciation

✤

I am grateful to the many well-wishers whose enthu-
siasm has encouraged me to develop this publication
from the original, among them, Bishop John Dough-
erty of Scranton, Pennsylvania; Msgr. Frank C. Wissel,
pastor of St. Mary's lovely church in Greenwich,
Connecticut; and especially that prolific Catholic
author, Msgr. Joseph M. Champlin, rector, Cathedral
of the Immaculate Conception, Syracuse, New York.

I have been privileged to donate my time and effort freely to this work, in thanksgiving to God for the
benefits of medical treatment and care I have received.
I donate all profit from any proceeds which might ac-
crue to me from this publication for the benefit of the
Missionaries of Charity, in honor of their founder the
late Mother Teresa, and as a tribute to the wonderful
work they perform in providing comfort for the poor
and the sick of this world, regardless of the religious
background or belief of those most in need.

JOHN MCQUIGGAN
CHRISTMAS 2002

Introduction

Many ministers of mercy to the sick or home-bound visit the same confined person or group of persons on a regular basis. They would appreciate a resource that could enrich these encounters by providing prayers and readings that may augment their visits. Other laypersons who visit the sick, and are conscious of their obligation for spiritual support to the members of their community, may wish for a simple self-contained series of prayer services that may be used on their visits. A veteran minister now gives them such a multiuse resource. He saw this need and compiled over fifty prayer services for use with the sick and homebound for this purpose.

Additionally, *A Time to Heal* contains the official ritual in the United States for the bringing of communion to the sick and homebound. Pastoral care of the sick stresses that those who are housebound through sickness, age, or other factors should have the opportunity to receive Communion frequently, even daily, and especially on Sunday. It would be practically impossible to implement that norm or ideal on the parish level without assistance from extraordinary ministers of the

Eucharist. Fortunately, over the past several decades a geometrically increasing number of Catholic men and women have come forward to volunteer their time and energy for this task.

In addition, *A Time to Heal* contains notes for visiting the sick, practical tips from author John McQuiggan developed from his own many years caring for the spiritual needs of infirm persons.

Originally published in the United Kingdom, this edition of *A Time to Heal* brings its riches to the United States with the hope that it can greatly enhance the ministry to the sick in this country.

FATHER JOSEPH M. CHAMPLIN, RECTOR
CATHEDRAL OF THE IMMACULATE CONCEPTION
SYRACUSE, NEW YORK

Notes for Visiting the Sick and the Homebound

Many people when using these prayer services employ a lighted candle as a symbol of enlightenment and the power of light over darkness. A candle might not be practical when making calls to hospital settings (candles are not welcomed in hospitals and some nursing homes because of the fire risk, and the sensitivity of any patients with breathing difficulties).

If, however, a candle is permissible and used, a brief prayer may be said at the time the candle is lit. Two such prayers are presented below.

Candle Prayers

Lord, by the light of this candle, through the prayers of Mary, Virgin and Mother, we place in your care those we pray for, especially *(insert name or names)*. Amen.

Lord, may this candle be a light for you to enlighten us in our difficulties and decisions. Amen.

Ensure that the people you are visiting know when you are coming. If you have an appointment and are unable to meet it, try to arrange for a substitute so that the recipients are not disappointed.

If you are unwell on the day, it is better to arrange for a substitute. The infirm and the sick are vulnerable, and you should not visit if the possibility exists that you might pass on an illness.

On arrival, look cheerful and greet the patient and anyone present, introduce yourself to anyone you do not already know. Be relaxed and friendly, this helps put everyone at ease. If appropriate, inquire about the patient's health out of courtesy, but avoid conversation on other topics until you finish the prayer service.

It is best to avoid involvement in medical matters, but listen politely if the patient wants to talk to you. Often the housebound can be very lonely and have a need to talk to somebody, so it is helpful to listen. If there appears to be a serious problem, consider referring it later to a relative or doctor. If you see a patient whose medical condition is deteriorating, you should inform the appropriate priest promptly.

Make best use of this book of services by commenting at the start of the service on the significance of the subject matter for that particular week. This will help the patient feel less isolated and more in touch with the main body of the Church.

As you leave, remember to thank the patient for allowing you the privilege of making the visit.

Prayer Services

Advent Week 1

Advent begins on the Sunday which falls on, or is closest to, November 30. Advent has four Sundays and, since the tenth century, has marked the beginning of the liturgical year for those following the Roman calendar. If possible, for this prayer service, arrange a small Advent wreath with four candles close by. Light one candle on the Advent wreath.

Greeting

The leader offers a greeting to all present.

May the grace of our Lord Jesus Christ,
and the love of God,
and the fellowship of the Holy Spirit
be with us all as we pray here together.
   R. Amen.

Gathering Prayer

The leader begins by saying this opening prayer.

All-powerful God, help us to take Christ's coming to heart. Increase our will to do good in any way that we are able so that Christ may find welcoming hearts at his coming. Through Christ our Lord.
   R. Amen.

First Reading

The leader reads a brief passage from sacred Scripture. This passage emphasizes the transience of life.

A reading from James 4:13–17

Here is the answer for those of you who talk like this:

"Today or tomorrow, we are off to this or that town; we are going to spend a year there, trading, and make some money."

You never know what will happen tomorrow; You are no more than a mist that is here for a little while and then disappears. The most you should ever say is: "If it is the Lord's will, we shall still be alive to do this or that."

But how proud and sure of yourselves you are now! Pride of this kind is always wicked. Everyone who knows what is the right thing to do and doesn't do it commits a sin.

R. The Word of the Lord.

Psalm 85:13–14

The leader prays a short selection from a psalm.

The Lord will give what is good,
and our land will yield its fruit.
Justice will go before him,
and peace will follow along his path.

Our Father

The leader introduces the Lord's Prayer.

Now let us pray together to the Father in the words given to us by his Son, our Lord Jesus Christ:

R. Our Father, who art in heaven,
   hallowed be thy name;
   thy kingdom come;
   thy will be done
   on earth as it is in heaven.
   Give us this day our daily bread,
   and forgive us our trespasses
   as we forgive those who trespass
   against us;
   and lead us not into temptation,
   but deliver us from evil.
   Amen.

Second Reading

The leader shares the following. A pause for meditation may be appropriate afterwards.

Humanity did not and could not have imagined that suffering rather than power might be a way of being for God. To know God from the standpoint of his suffering on the cross is to abide with God in his Passion.

JON SOBRINO

Prayer for Those Who Suffer

For all who have suffered
an unspeakable loss,
for those who have to go on living alone
after the death of their partner, and
for those whose hearts ache after the death
of a child, a friend, or close relative,
O Lord, hear our prayer.
We ask this in the name of Jesus, our Lord.

   R. Amen.

Let us remember in these prayers all who are sick
and in need, our doctors, nurses, and caregivers, our
relatives and friends, living and dead, and the souls of
all those recently deceased, as we seek the intercession
of the Holy Mother of God, and say together:

R. Hail Mary, full of grace,
the Lord is with thee.
Blessed art thou among women
and blessed is the fruit of
thy womb Jesus.
Holy Mary, Mother of God,
pray for us sinners,
now and at the hour of our death.
Amen.

Prayer for Christ's Company in Suffering

After making the sign of the cross, the leader says this final prayer.

May the Lord be our strength
as we struggle through our suffering.
May the Lord be our eyes so that we can see
our way through our emotional and physical pain.
May the Lord be at our feet on this journey,
so we may be carried forward in his love.
May we always be aware that the Lord
walks beside us
and, as did Simon of Cyrene on Calvary,
help us carry our cross of suffering.
    R. Amen.

The leader concludes by saying to those present:

May the Lord be with you always,
to be your strength and your peace.
    R. Thanks be to God.

Advent Week 2

For this prayer service, set up a small Advent wreath close by. Light two candles on the Advent wreath.

Greeting

The leader offers a greeting to all present.

May the grace of our Lord Jesus Christ,
and the love of God,
and the fellowship of the Holy Spirit
be with us all as we pray here together.
    R. Amen.

Gathering Prayer

The leader begins with this prayer.

Let us pray for the arrival of the Savior. May our hearts rise in welcome, and may our suffering not prevent us from savoring the joy of his coming. We ask you this in the name of Jesus, our Lord.
    R. Amen.

First Reading

The leader reads a brief passage from sacred Scripture. This text tells about the baptism of Jesus by John the Baptist.

A reading from the Gospel of John 1:29–34

The next day, seeing Jesus coming towards him, John said, "Look, there is the Lamb of God that takes away the sin of the world. This is the one I spoke of when I said: A man is coming after me who ranks before me because he existed before me.

"I did not know him myself, and yet it was to reveal him to Israel that I came baptizing with water." John also declared, "I saw the Spirit coming down on him from heaven like a dove and resting on him. I did not know him myself, but he who sent me to baptize with water had said to me, 'The man on whom you see the Spirit come down and rest is the one who is going to baptize with the Holy Spirit.' Yes, I have seen and I am the witness that he is the Chosen One of God."

R. The Gospel of the Lord.

Psalm 85:5, 7–8

The leader prays a brief psalm.

God our savior…will you not give us life anew,
that your people may rejoice in you?
Show us, O Lord, your unfailing love
and grant us your saving help.

Our Father

The leader introduces the Lord's Prayer.

With trust in God who heals and supports us, we now pray as Jesus taught us:

R. *Our Father, who art in heaven,*
hallowed be thy name,
thy kingdom come,
thy will be done,
on earth as it is in heaven.
Give us this day our daily bread,
and forgive us our trespasses
as we forgive those who trespass
against us;
and lead us not into temptation,
but deliver us from evil.
Amen.

Second Reading

The leader reads this short quotation.

We cannot shed a tear, but that tear has already blinded the eyes of Christ...He has known all and every kind of fear that we know, and there is no possible loneliness, no agony of separation, but it is Christ's; indeed, not one of us can die, but it is Christ dying. And Christ, Who faces all these things in our lives, has overcome them all.

CARYLL HOUSELANDER

Prayer for Our Needs

The leader prays on behalf of all present.

God, our Father,
we ask for your care and protection.
Your love never fails.
Hear our call. Keep us from danger
and provide for all our needs.
We ask this through our Lord Jesus Christ.
   R. *Amen.*

Let us remember in these prayers all who are sick
and in need, our doctors, nurses, and caregivers, our
relatives and friends, living and dead, and the souls of
all those recently deceased, as we seek the intercession
of the Holy Mother of God, and say together:

R. *Hail Mary, full of grace,*
   the Lord is with thee.
   Blessed art thou among women,
   and blessed is the fruit
   of thy womb Jesus.
   Holy Mary, Mother of God,
   pray for us sinners now
   and at the hour of our death.
   Amen.

Prayer for God's Healing Power

After making the sign of the cross, the leader says this final prayer.

Heavenly Father,
pour out your Spirit upon us your people
as we come together in your name.
Grant us a new vision of your glory—
a new experience of your power—
a new faithfulness to your word—
a new dedication to your service—
as we celebrate your presence among us.
May we together proclaim the good news of Christ,
and transform the world with his love—
so that all may come to your Kingdom—
where you live forever and ever.
 R. *Amen.*

The leader concludes by saying to those present:

May the Lord be with you always,
to be your strength and your peace.
 R. *Thanks be to God.*

Advent Week 3

For this prayer service, set up a small Advent wreath close by. Light three candles on the Advent wreath.

Greeting

The leader offers a greeting to all present.

May the peace of our Lord Jesus Christ,
and the love of God, his Father,
and the inspiration of the Holy Spirit
be with us all as we pray here together.
   R. Amen.

Gathering Prayer

The leader begins by saying this opening prayer.

Let us pray that we may find joy and hope and healing in the coming of our Savior. May we look forward with longing to that time when we shall rejoice with all the saints at the heavenly banquet that God has prepared for us. We ask this through Christ our Lord.
   R. Amen.

First Reading

The leader reads a brief passage from sacred Scripture. This passage tells about God's overwhelming love for his people.

A reading from 1 John 4:7–12

My dear people,
let us love one another
since love comes from God
and everyone who loves is begotten by God and
    knows God.
Anyone who fails to love can never have known God,
because God is love.
God's love for us was revealed
when God sent into the world his only Son
so that we could have life through him;
this is the love I mean: not our love for God,
but God's love for us when he sent his Son
to be the sacrifice that takes our sins away.
My dear people,
since God has loved us so much,
we too should love one another.
No one has ever seen God;
but as long as we love one another
God will live in us
and his love will be complete in us.
    R. The Word of the Lord.

Psalm 80:2–3

The leader prays a brief psalm.

Listen, O shepherd of Israel…
you who sit enthroned between the cherubim,
stir up your might and come to save us.

Our Father

The leader introduces the Lord's Prayer.

With trust in God who heals and supports us, we now pray as Jesus taught us:

> *R. Our Father, who art in heaven,*
> *hallowed be thy name;*
> *thy kingdom come;*
> *thy will be done*
> *on earth as it is in heaven.*
> *Give us this day our daily bread,*
> *and forgive us our trespasses,*
> *as we forgive those who trespass*
> *against us;*
> *and lead us not into temptation,*
> *but deliver us from evil.*
> *Amen.*

Second Reading

The leader reads the following quotation.

Justly does the Apostle call Jesus Christ our life. Behold our Redeemer, clothed with flesh and become an Infant, and saying to us, "I have come that you might have life and have it to the full."

SAINT ALPHONSUS LIGUORI

Prayer for Unselfishness

The leader offers a prayer for those present.

God our Father,
we rejoice in the faith that draws us together,
aware that selfishness can drive us apart.
Let your encouragement be our constant strength.
Keep us one in the love that has sealed our lives,
help us to live as one family
the Gospel we profess.
We ask this through Christ our Lord.
    R. Amen.

Let us remember in these prayers all who are sick and in need, our doctors, nurses, and caregivers, all our relatives and friends, living and dead, and the souls of those recently deceased, as we seek the intercession of the Holy Mother of God, and say together:

> *R. Hail Mary, full of grace,*
> *the Lord is with thee.*
> *Blessed art thou among women,*
> *and blessed is the fruit*
> *of thy womb Jesus.*
> *Holy Mary, Mother of God,*
> *pray for us sinners now*
> *and at the hour of our death.*
> *Amen.*

Prayer for a Cure for Suffering

After the assembly makes the sign of the cross, the leader says this final prayer.

If you wish it, Lord,
you can save me from suffering
or you can cure me.
I do not understand why you don't do something,
but if this is your will, so be it.

You bore the pain of the cross;
please help me to bear this agony.
God of goodness, stay with me,
so that I shall not lose my way in this suffering.
I ask this through our Lord Jesus Christ.
    R. Amen.

The leader concludes by saying to those present:

May the Lord be with you always,
to be your strength and your peace.
    R. Thanks be to God.

Advent Week 4

For this prayer service, if possible, set up a small Advent wreath close by. Light four candles on the Advent wreath.

Greeting

The leader offers a greeting to all present.

Lord Jesus Christ, may your peace
and the love of God, your Father,
and the wisdom of the Holy Spirit,
be with us all as we pray here together.
    R. Amen.

Gathering Prayer

The leader begins by saying this opening prayer.

Let us pray: Lord, all-powerful, who became flesh among us when the Virgin Mary said her "yes" to the angel, keep our minds open to receive the One who comes and infuse our lives with the Holy Spirit.
    R. Amen.

First Reading

The leader reads a brief passage from sacred Scripture. This passage tells us about compassion.

A reading from the Letter of Paul to Titus 3:4–8

When the kindness and love of God our Savior for mankind was revealed, it was not because he was concerned with any righteous actions we might have done ourselves; it was for no reason except his own compassion that he saved us, by means of the cleansing water of rebirth and by renewing us with the Holy Spirit which he has so generously poured over us through Jesus Christ our Savior. He did this so that we should be justified by his grace, to become heirs looking forward to inheriting eternal life.

R. The Word of the Lord.

Psalm 145:18–19

The leader prays an excerpt from a psalm.

The Lord is near those who call trustfully on him;
He fulfills the wish of those who fear him;
He hears their cry and saves them.

Our Father

The leader introduces the Lord's Prayer.

With trust in God who heals and supports us, we now pray as Jesus taught us:

R. Our Father, who art in heaven,
hallowed be thy name;
thy kingdom come;
thy will be done on earth as it is in heaven.

Give us this day our daily bread,
and forgive us our trespasses
as we forgive those who trespass
against us;
lead us not into temptation,
but deliver us from evil.
Amen.

Second Reading

The leader shares this brief quotation.

What happiness it is that in death we ought not to rely on anything we have done or services we have rendered, but solely on God's boundless goodness and grace. There is no other fire than that of the love of God which purifies us and brings to perfection what is imperfect.

FRANCIS BOURDEAU

Prayer in the Face of Tension and Change

The leader continues with this prayer for those present.

Lord, when we face any change in life,
we begin to deal with it
by continuing to function in the way
that we have done before the change occurred.
When that doesn't work any more, we face tension
until we accept that our previous way of coping
is no longer effective.

To deal with change and to grow through it,
we have to find new ways of coping;
new ways of living.
Lord, help us to find these new ways.
   R. Amen.

   Let us remember in these prayers all who are sick
and in need, our doctors, nurses, and caregivers, all our
relatives and friends, living and dead, and the souls of
all those recently deceased, as we seek the intercession
of the Holy Mother of God, and say together:

   R. Hail Mary, full of grace,
   the Lord is with thee.
   Blessed art thou among women,
   and blessed is the fruit
   of thy womb Jesus.
   Holy Mary, Mother of God,
   pray for us sinners now
   and at the hour of our death.
   Amen.

Prayer for Healing

After the assembly makes the sign of the cross, the leader
says this final prayer.

I felt your healing touch the other day—
Not in my body but in my soul,
The hurt and needs and fears all disappeared—
Your healing touch had made me free and whole.

I felt your healing touch the other day
In both my spirit and my soul—
And joy and faith and love rose in my heart—
Your healing touch had made my spirit whole.

I need your healing touch this very day
Here in my body, not in my soul;
I ask according to your precious word—
Your healing touch to make me fully whole.
  R. Amen.

The leader concludes by saying to those present:

May the Lord be with you always,
to be your strength and your peace.
  R. *Thanks be to God.*

Christmas Day

The Christmas season begins with the vigil of Christmas and lasts until the Sunday after Epiphany, or after January 6, inclusive. If possible, for this prayer service, set up a small crèche or bring photos of the Christmas activities in your local church to share.

Greeting

The leader offers a greeting to all present.

May the grace of our Lord Jesus Christ,
and the love of God,
and the fellowship of the Holy Spirit
be with us all as we pray here together.
    R. *Amen.*

Gathering Prayer

The leader says this opening prayer.

Let us pray that we may celebrate the birthday of the Prince of Peace with wonder and joy at the nearness of our Lord.

A child is born to us and a son is given us. May our hearts receive him joyfully.
    R. *Amen.*

First Reading

The leader reads a brief passage from sacred Scripture. This passage recounts the glory and praise of the shepherds at our Lord's birth.

A reading from the Gospel according to Luke 2:15–20

Now when the angels had gone from them into heaven, the shepherds said to one another, "Let us go to Bethlehem and see this thing that has happened which the Lord has made known to us." So they hurried away and found Mary and Joseph, and the baby lying in the manger. When they saw the child they repeated what they had been told about him, and everyone who heard it was astonished at what the shepherds had to say. As for Mary, she treasured all these things and pondered them in her heart. And the shepherds went back glorifying and praising God for all they had heard and seen.

R. *The Gospel of the Lord.*

Psalm 2:7

The leader prays a brief excerpt from a psalm.

I will proclaim the decree of the Lord.
He said to me: "You are my son.
This day I have begotten you."

Our Father

The leader introduces the Lord's Prayer.

Now let us pray together to the Father in the words given to us by his Son, our Lord Jesus Christ:

> *R. Our Father, who art in heaven,*
> *hallowed be thy name,*
> *thy kingdom come,*
> *thy will be done,*
> *on earth as it is in heaven.*
> *Give us this day our daily bread,*
> *and forgive us our trespasses*
> *as we forgive those who trespass*
> *against us;*
> *and lead us not into temptation,*
> *but deliver us from evil.*
> *Amen.*

Second Reading

The leader shares this brief quotation.

The mystery of Christmas is not a reality *outside* of you. It is realized only if it becomes a reality *within* you. Mary and Joseph sought shelter. And the King of Kings was satisfied with a poor stable and manger meant for cattle. Is there a shelter for him within you—he doesn't ask for much—or are you so preoccupied with your own well-being that there is no room for him? If you let Jesus be born in you, you become a messenger of love. Then you will no longer do anything just for your own sake. Everything you do will be inspired by love.

WILFRID STINISSEN, O. CARM.

Prayer of Joy

The leader shares this prayer with those present.

Let us sing a new song for the Lord,
his praise in the assembly of the faithful.
Let Israel rejoice in its Maker,
Let Zion's sons exult in their king.
Let them all praise his name with dancing
and make music with timbrel and harp.

For the Lord takes delight in his people.
He crowns the poor with salvation.
Let the faithful rejoice in their glory,
shout loud for joy and take their rest.
Let the praise of God be on their lips.

Let us remember in these prayers all who are sick and in need, and our doctors, nurses, and caregivers, all our relatives and friends, living and dead, and the souls of all those recently deceased, as we seek the intercession of the Holy Mother of God, and say together:

R. *Hail Mary, full of grace,*
the Lord is with thee.
Blessed art thou among women
and blessed is the fruit of
thy womb Jesus.
Holy Mary, Mother of God,
pray for us sinners,
now and at the hour of our death.
Amen.

Sign of Peace

After the assembly makes the sign of the cross, the leader suggests the following.

Saint Alphonsus wrote, "Joy awoke at Jesus' birth and roamed creation free." In the joy of the Word-Made-Flesh, let us offer to one another a sign of Christmas joy and peace.

R. *Amen.*

The leader concludes by saying to those present:

May the Lord be with you always,
to be your strength and your peace.

R. *Thanks be to God.*

Holy Family

The movable feast of the Holy Family is celebrated on the Sunday within eight days (octave) of Christmas; if no Sunday occurs within the octave, then this feast is observed on December 30. You may wish to bring news of needy families who have received help at Christmas to this prayer service.

Greeting

The leader offers a greeting to all present.

May the grace of our Lord Jesus Christ,
and the love of God,
and the fellowship of the Holy Spirit,
be with us all as we pray here together.
    R. Amen.

Gathering Prayer

The leader begins by saying this opening prayer.

Let us pray, Father of us all, teach us how to live as did the Holy Family, consecrated in love, joy, and peace, and helped by the obedient example of the young Jesus.
    R. Amen.

First Reading

The leader reads a passage from sacred Scripture. In this passage, Christ announces that we are his sons and daughters, not slaves.

A reading from the Letter of Paul to the Galatians 4:4–7

When the appointed time came, God sent his Son, born of a woman, born a subject of the Law, to redeem the subjects of the Law and to enable us to be adopted as sons. The proof that you are sons is that God has sent the Spirit of his Son into our hearts: the Spirit that cries, "Abba, Father," and it is this that makes you a son. You are not a slave any more; and if God has made you a son, then he has made you heir.

R. The Word of the Lord.

Psalm 27:4

The leader prays a brief psalm.

One thing I ask of the Lord...
that I may dwell in his house
all the days of my life.

Our Father

The leader introduces the Lord's Prayer.

With trust in God who heals and supports us, we now pray as Jesus taught us:

R. Our Father, who art in heaven,
hallowed be thy name;
thy kingdom come;
thy will be done
on earth as it is in heaven.
Give us this day our daily bread,
and forgive us our trespasses,
as we forgive those who trespass
against us,
and lead us not into temptation,
but deliver us from evil.
Amen.

Second Reading

The leader shares this brief quotation.

Death is a passage to new life. That sounds very beautiful, but few of us desire to make this passage. It might be helpful to realize that our final passage is preceded by many earlier passages. When we are born we make a passage from life in the womb to life in the family. When we go to school we make a passage from life in the family to life in the larger community. When we get married we make a passage from a life with many options to a life committed to one person....Each of these passages is a death leading to new life. When we live these passages well, we are becoming more prepared for our final passage.

Henri Nouwen

Prayer to the God of Love

The leader shares this prayer with those present.

Let us pray,
God of love to all peoples and
our Father in Heaven,
the perfection of justice is found in your love
and all humankind is in need of your law.
Help us to find this love in each other,
that justice may be attained
through obedience to your law.
We ask this through Christ our Lord.

    R. Amen.

Let us remember in these prayers all who are sick and in need, our doctors, nurses, and caregivers, all our relatives and friends, living and dead, and the souls of all those recently deceased, as we seek the intercession of the Holy Mother of God, and say together:

    R. Hail Mary, full of grace,
       the Lord is with thee.
       Blessed art thou among women,
       and blessed is the fruit
       of thy womb Jesus.
       Holy Mary, Mother of God,
       pray for us sinners now
       and at the hour of our death.
       Amen.

Prayer for the Family

Those assembled make the sign of the cross, and the leader says this final prayer.

Let us pray,
O dear Jesus, we humbly implore you
to grant your special graces to this family.
May our home be the shrine of peace, purity,
   love, labor, and faith.
We beg you, dear Jesus,
to protect and bless all of us,
absent and present, living and dead.
May the blessing of almighty God,
Father, Son, and Holy Spirit, come down upon us,
and protect us from all evil and harm.
   R. Amen.

The leader concludes by saying to those present:

May the Lord be with you always,
to be your strength and your peace.
   R. Thanks be to God.

Solemnity of Mary, Mother of God

This holy day of obligation is observed on January 1. You may wish to bring along a small icon of Mary for this prayer service.

Greeting

The leader offers a greeting to all present.

May the grace of our Lord Jesus Christ,
the love of God,
and the fellowship of the Holy Spirit,
be with us all as we pray here together.
  R. Amen.

Gathering Prayer

The leader begins by saying this opening prayer.

We ask you, O Lord, to pour forth on us your grace so that we, to whom the Incarnation of Christ your Son was made known by the message of an angel, may by his passion and cross, be brought to the glory of his Resurrection.
  R. Amen.

First Reading

The leader reads a passage from sacred Scripture. This text reminds us of Mary's calm acceptance of God's will for her.

A reading from the Gospel according to Luke 2:16–21

The shepherds hurried away to Bethlehem and found Mary and Joseph, and the baby lying in the manger. When they saw the child they repeated what they had been told about him, and everyone who heard it was astonished at what the shepherds had to say. As for Mary, she treasured all these things and pondered them in her heart. And the shepherds went back glorifying and praising God for all they had heard and seen; it was exactly as they had been told. When the eighth day came and the child was to be circumcised, they gave him the name Jesus, the name the angel had given him before his conception.

R. *The Gospel of the Lord.*

Psalm 44:14–15

The leader prays a brief psalm.

All glorious as she enters
is the princess in her gold-woven robes.
She is led in royal attire to the king,
following behind is her train of virgins.

Our Father

The leader introduces the Lord's Prayer.

We commend all whom we love, or who have been entrusted to our prayers, to the unfailing love of God, and say together, as Christ himself has taught us:

> **R.** *Our Father, who art in heaven,*
> *hallowed be thy name;*
> *thy kingdom come;*
> *thy will be done*
> *on earth as it is in heaven.*
> *Give us this day our daily bread,*
> *and forgive us our trespasses,*
> *as we forgive those who trespass*
> *against us,*
> *and lead us not into temptation,*
> *but deliver us from evil.*
> *Amen.*

Second Reading

The leader reads this brief quotation.

Mary witnesses to the value of a humble and hidden life. Everyone usually demands, and sometimes almost claims, to be able to realize fully his or her own person and qualities. Everyone is sensitive to esteem and honor....Mary, on the contrary, never sought honor or the advantages of a privileged position. She always tried to fulfill God's will, leading a life according to the

Father's plan of salvation. To all those who often feel the burden of a seemingly insignificant life, Mary reveals how valuable life can be if it is lived for love of Christ.

POPE JOHN PAUL II

Prayer to Our Lady

The leader invites our Lady's intercessions as we pray.

Most blessed Virgin Mary, who under the shadow and power of the Holy Spirit, prepared in your spotless womb, a fit dwelling place for the Incarnate Word of God, intercede for us now so that, by the power of the same Holy Spirit, we may be purified of our sins and worthy of eternal peace with our Lord and Savior.
R. *Amen.*

Let us remember in these prayers all who are sick and in need, our doctors, nurses, caregivers, all our relatives and friends, living and dead, and the souls of all those recently deceased, as we seek the intercession of the Holy Mother of God, and say together:

> **R.** *Hail Mary, full of grace,*
> *the Lord is with thee.*
> *Blessed art thou among women*
> *and blessed is the fruit of thy womb Jesus.*
> *Holy Mary, Mother of God,*
> *pray for us sinners,*
> *now and at the hour of our death.*
> *Amen.*

Prayer for Shared Suffering

After the assembly makes the sign of the cross, the leader says this prayer.

God our Father, when Jesus your Son was crucified on the cross, it was your will that Mary, his Mother, should stand there and suffer in her heart with him. Grant that in union with her, we may share in the passion of Christ, and so be brought to the glory of his Resurrection. We make our prayer through Christ our Lord.

R. Amen.

The leader concludes by saying to those present:

May the Lord be with you always,
to be your strength and your peace.
    R. Thanks be to God.

Epiphany

The solemnity of the Epiphany commemorating the homage of the Wise Men from the East is observed on January 6. It may be appropriate to bring with you three small gold crowns as reminders of the three kings.

Greeting

The leader offers a greeting to all present.

May the grace of our Lord Jesus Christ,
and the love of God,
and the fellowship of the Holy Spirit,
be with us all as we pray here together.
    R. Amen.

Gathering Prayer

The leader begins by saying this opening prayer.

Behold our Savior has come. May the star of our faith guide us to you, O Lord. We offer you our unceasing praise to the glory of God the Father.
    R. Amen.

First Reading

The leader reads a passage from sacred Scripture. This text reminds us that Christ is the Light of the World.

A reading from the Book of Isaiah 60:1–2

Arise, shine out, for your light has come,
the glory of the Lord is rising on you,
though night still covers the earth
and darkness the peoples.

> R. *The Word of the Lord.*

Psalm 72:1, 15

The leader prays a brief psalm.

O God, endow the king with your justice,
the royal son with your righteousness....
May he live long,
may gold from Sheba be given him.

Our Father

The leader introduces the Lord's Prayer.

We commend all whom we love, or who have been
entrusted to our prayers, to the unfailing love of God,
and say together, as Christ himself has taught us:

> R. *Our Father, who art in heaven,*
> *hallowed be thy name;*
> *thy kingdom come;*
> *thy will be done*
> *on earth as it is in heaven.*
> *Give us this day our daily bread,*
> *and forgive us our trespasses*

as we forgive those who trespass
against us;
and lead us not into temptation,
but deliver us from evil.
Amen.

Second Reading

The leader reads this brief quotation.

God accepts those who come in faith, bringing nothing but a confession of sin. And this is the highest excellence to which we ordinarily attain; to understand our own hypocrisy, insincerity, and shallowness of mind—and to submit ourselves wholly to his judgment, who could indeed be extreme with us, but who has already shown his loving-kindness in bidding us to pray. And while we thus conduct ourselves, we must learn to feel that God knows all this before we say it, far better than we do.

FULTON J. SHEEN

A Prayer for a New Day

The leader shares this prayer with those present.

Let us pray,
O God, thank you for sleep,
and for all who have looked after us
during the night.
Thank you for this new day and the promise
of your peace.

Help us this day in our weakness to discover
     your strength,
help us to face discomfort without complaining,
to bear pain if need be with courage,
to be as helpful and considerate as we can
to other patients and to the staff.

O God, we want the courage to go through this day
     with our hand in yours.
Let your encouragement be our constant strength.
Keep us in the love that has sealed our lives,
and help us to live as one Gospel family,
the faith that we profess.
We ask this through Christ our Lord.
     R. Amen.

Let us remember in these prayers all who are sick
and in need, our doctors, nurses, and caregivers, all our
relatives and friends, living and dead, and the souls of
all those recently deceased, as we seek the intercession
of the Holy Mother of God, and say together:

> *R. Hail Mary, full of grace,*
> *the Lord is with thee.*
> *Blessed art thou among women*
> *and blessed is the fruit of*
> *thy womb Jesus.*
> *Holy Mary, Mother of God,*
> *pray for us sinners,*
> *now and at the hour of our death.*
> *Amen.*

Act of Worship

After the assembly makes the sign of the cross, the leader says this prayer.

Lord, I will worship you
In the gentleness of the rain,
In the power of the storm,
And in the beauty of a single flower.
I will worship you in the silence of the dawn,
And in the turmoil of our noisy lives.
I will worship you in this place,
And in every place that you dwell.
And I pray that my every thought, word, and action
may be a hymn to the glory of you my God.

The leader concludes by saying to those present:

May the Lord be with you always,
to be your strength and your peace.
    R. Thanks be to God.

Baptism of Our Lord

A movable feast, this celebration falls on the Sunday after January 6.

Greeting

The leader offers a greeting to all present.

May the grace of our Lord Jesus Christ,
and the love of God,
and the fellowship of the Holy Spirit
be with us all as we pray here together.
> R. Amen.

Gathering Prayer

The leader begins by saying this opening prayer.

We ask you, almighty God, that we, who have been baptized in the name of your Son, may follow your will for us and live a worthy life in your sight.
> R. Amen.

First Reading

The leader reads a passage from sacred Scripture. This text tells us that humility is needed to enter the kingdom of heaven.

A reading from the Gospel according to
Matthew 18:1–5

The disciples came to Jesus and said, "Who is the greatest in the kingdom of heaven?" So he called a little child to him and set the child in front of them. Then he said, "I tell you solemnly, unless you change and become like little children you will never enter the kingdom of heaven. And so, the one who makes himself as small as this little child is the greatest in the kingdom of heaven. Anyone who welcomes a little child like this in my name welcomes me."
R. The Gospel of the Lord.

Psalm 101:1–2

The leader prays a brief psalm.

I will sing of your love and justice;
to you, O Lord, I will sing praise.
I will walk the way of integrity—
O Lord, when will you come to me?

Our Father

The leader introduces the Lord's Prayer.

We commend all whom we love, or who have been entrusted to our prayers, to the unfailing love of God, and say together, as Christ himself has taught us:

R. *Our Father, who art in heaven,*
   hallowed be thy name;
   thy kingdom come;
   thy will be done
   on earth as it is in heaven.
   Give us this day our daily bread,
   and forgive us our trespasses
   as we forgive those who trespass
   against us,
   And lead us not into temptation,
   but deliver us from evil.
   Amen.

Second Reading

The leader reads this brief quotation.

We must hold our hearts open towards heaven and never forget that in prayer we approach God and put ourselves in his presence for two main reasons. The first is to render God the honor and homage which we owe him, and this can be done without him speaking to us or ourselves speaking to him. The second reason for which we present ourselves before God is to speak to him and hear him speak to us by inner stirrings of the heart…, and it is of very great benefit for us to speak to so great a Lord, and when he answers he pours out balm and much precious ointment to fill our soul with sweetness.

SAINT FRANCIS DE SALES

Prayer for Life

The leader shares this prayer with those present.

The law of the Lord is perfect,
it revives the soul.
The precepts of the Lord are right,
they gladden the heart.
> *R. Your words are spirit, Lord, and they are life.*

The fear of the Lord is holy,
abiding forever.
The decrees of the Lord are truth
and all of them just.
> *R. Your words are spirit, Lord, and they are life.*

May the spoken words of my mouth,
the thoughts of my heart,
win favor in your sight, O Lord,
my rescuer, my rock!
> *R. Your words are spirit, Lord, and they are life.*

Let us remember in these prayers all who are sick and in need, our doctors, nurses, caregivers, all our relatives and friends, living and dead, and the souls of all those recently deceased, as we seek the intercession of the Holy Mother of God, and say together:

> *R. Hail Mary, full of grace,*
> *the Lord is with thee.*
> *Blessed art thou among women*
> *and blessed is the fruit of*
> *thy womb Jesus.*

Holy Mary, Mother of God,
pray for us sinners,
now and at the hour of our death.
Amen.

Prayer to the Holy Spirit

Those assembled make the sign of the cross, and the leader says this final prayer.

God our loving Father, send your Holy Spirit to bring forth Christ, our Light, to this place. Help us to remember, Lord, that only you can make all things new, and that we are here to do your will. Renew in us what is weary and worn, and restore what has been lost. Give us hearts strong with hope and confident in your love. Fill us anew with your gifts: forgiveness, love, and healing, especially so that others may know and love you.

   R. *Amen.*

The leader concludes by saying to those present:

May the Lord be with you always,
to be your strength and your peace.

   R. *Thanks be to God.*

Week of Prayer for Christian Unity

This observance is comprised of eight days of prayer, from January 18 to January 25, for the union of all persons in the Church established by Christ.

Greeting

The leader offers a greeting to all present.

May the grace of our Lord Jesus Christ,
and the love of God,
and the fellowship of the Holy Spirit,
be with us all as we pray here together.
   R. *Amen.*

Gathering Prayer

The leader begins by saying this opening prayer.

God, our Father, who has communicated your wisdom to us by means of Jesus, his words and deeds, may we also join with all who have accepted the Word of God, and achieve understanding hearts and common bonds. Through Christ our Lord.
   R. *Amen.*

First Reading

The leader reads a passage from sacred Scripture. This text proclaims the universality of the Church.

A reading according to the Gospel of John 17:18–21

As you sent me into the world,
I have sent them into the world,
and for their sake I consecrate myself
so that they too may be consecrated in truth.
I pray not only for these,
but for those also
who through their words will believe in me.
May they all be one.

> R. *The Gospel of the Lord.*

Psalm 133:1–3

The leader prays a brief psalm.

Where brothers and sisters dwell in unity,
there the Lord commands his blessings.
How good it is when all live together in unity!
It is like precious oil poured on the head.

Our Father

The leader introduces the Lord's Prayer.

We commend all whom we love, or who have been
entrusted to our prayers, to the unfailing love of God,
and say together, as Christ himself has taught us:

> R. *Our Father, who art in heaven,*
> *hallowed be thy name;*
> *thy kingdom come;*
> *thy will be done on earth as it is in heaven.*

Give us this day our daily bread,
and forgive us our trespasses
as we forgive those who trespass
against us,
and lead us not into temptation,
but deliver us from evil.
Amen.

Second Reading

The leader reads this brief quotation.

Many people try to develop their lives by multiplied contacts, expanding reputation, vaster possessions. The true value of life does not lie on the surface, but at a depth. It is not measured by quantity but by quality. We often complain of our powerlessness in the face of events. We have no right to do so unless we have first exhausted all the capabilities within us. When we have done that, we shall perceive that these capabilities grow with their exercise, that one may always surpass oneself.

A. G. SERTILLANGES, O.P.

Prayer to the Holy Spirit

The leader shares this prayer with those present.

Heavenly Father,
pour out your spirit on us, your people,
as we come together in your name.

Grant us a new vision of your glory—
a new experience of your power—
a new awareness of your love—
as we celebrate your presence among us.
Show us the way to unity and faith and worship
with all those who accept Jesus as their Savior.
May we together proclaim the Good News
    of Salvation,
and transform the world with his love—
so that all may come to your Kingdom,
where you live and reign forever and ever.
    R. Amen.

Let us remember in these prayers all who are sick
and in need, our doctors, nurses, and caregivers, all our
relatives and friends, living and dead, and the souls of
all those recently deceased, as we seek the intercession
of the Holy Mother of God, and say together:

R. Hail Mary, full of grace,
    the Lord is with thee.
    Blessed art thou among women
    and blessed is the fruit of
    thy womb Jesus.
    Holy Mary, Mother of God,
    pray for us sinners,
    now and at the hour of our death.
    Amen.

Prayer for Christian Unity

After the assembly makes the sign of the cross, the leader says this final prayer for Christian Unity.

O God, our Father—
source of all that is good—
in you is all truth, peace, and harmony.
Among those who are Christian,
heal what divides us from one another—
bring us back to that unity of love, faith, and
worship, which you desire—
so that we become one flock with you our shepherd.

Make us one in the spirit
through that love and peace,
which makes all things beautiful in your sight.
We make our prayer through the grace and mercy
of him who died for us all—
your son Jesus Christ, our Lord.
　　R. Amen.

The leader concludes by saying to those present:

May the Lord be with you always,
to be your strength and your peace.
　　R. Thanks be to God.

Presentation of Our Lord

This feast, also called Candlemas in some places, is observed on February 2 and commemorates the presentation of Jesus in the Temple and the purification of his mother, Mary, forty days after his birth. This is the day on which church candles are generally blessed. The candle is a symbol of light.

Greeting

The leader offers a greeting to all present.

May the grace of our Lord Jesus Christ,
and the love of God,
and the fellowship of the Holy Spirit,
be with us all as we pray here together.
> *R. Amen.*

Gathering Prayer

The leader begins by saying this opening prayer.

Let us take the Christ Child into our hearts, as Simeon took him into his arms when his parents brought the infant to the Temple according to the law. May the grace of our Lord light our life.
> *R. Amen.*

First Reading

The leader reads a passage from sacred Scripture. This text relates that our God is one of light.

A reading from the Gospel according to John 1:1–14

In the beginning was the Word, and the Word was with God; and the Word *was* God.

He was in the beginning with God.

All things were made through him, and without him was made nothing that has been made.

In him was life, and the life was the light of men.

And the light shines in the darkness; and the darkness grasped it not.

There was a man, one sent by God, whose name was John. This man came as a witness, to bear witness concerning the light, that all might believe through him.

He was not himself the light, but was to bear witness to the light.

It was the true light that enlightens every man who comes into the world. He was in the world, and the world was made through him, and the world knew him not. He came unto his own, and his own received him not.

But to as many as received him he gave the power of becoming sons of God; to those who believe in his name: who were born not of blood, nor of the will of the flesh, nor of the will of man, but of God. And the Word was made flesh, and dwelt among us.

R. The Gospel of the Lord.

Psalm 48:10–11, 15

The leader prays a brief psalm.

Let us recall your unfailing love,
O God, inside your temple.
Let your praise as does your name, O God,
reach to the ends of the earth.
Your right hand is ever victorious....
God is our guide forever.
    R. Amen.

Our Father

The leader introduces the Lord's Prayer.

We commend all whom we love, or who have been
entrusted to our prayers, to the unfailing love of God,
and say together, as Christ himself has taught us:

> *R. Our Father, who art in heaven,*
> *hallowed be thy name;*
> *thy kingdom come;*
> *thy will be done*
> *on earth as it is in heaven.*
> *Give us this day our daily bread,*
> *and forgive us our trespasses,*
> *as we forgive those who trespass*
> *against us,*
> *and lead us not into temptation,*
> *but deliver us from evil.*
> *Amen.*

Second Reading

The leader reads this brief quotation.

All suffering is difficult. But all suffering can be united with the suffering of Christ on the cross to bring great good into the world, to help save souls, including our own. Suffering can embitter or ennoble. Suffering can demean or dignify. Suffering can corrode or purify….It is not that understanding the power of suffering makes the suffering itself less difficult; it's that it makes it more meaningful.

JOHN CARDINAL O'CONNOR

A Prayer for Our Family

The leader shares this prayer with those present.

Hear us, O Lord,
on behalf of those who are dear to us,
all whom we have in mind at this moment.

Be near them in all their anxieties and worries.
Give them the help of your saving grace.
We commend them all with trustful confidence
to your merciful love.

Remember, Lord,
all who have asked us to pray for them,
all who have been kind to us;
all who have wronged us,
or whom we have wronged
by ill-will or by misunderstanding.

Give all of us grace to bear each other's faults,
and to share each other's burdens.
Have mercy on the souls of our loved ones
who have gone before us,
and grant them peace and happiness.
      R. Amen.

Let us remember in these prayers all who are sick
and in need, our doctors, nurses, and caregivers, all our
relatives and friends, living and dead, and the souls of
all those recently deceased, as we seek the intercession
of the Holy Mother of God, and say together:

> *R. Hail Mary, full of grace,*
> *the Lord is with thee.*
> *Blessed art thou among women*
> *and blessed is the fruit of*
> *thy womb Jesus.*
> *Holy Mary, Mother of God,*
> *pray for us sinners,*
> *now and at the hour of our death.*
> *Amen.*

Prayer for Faith

After the assembly makes the sign of the cross, the leader
says this prayer.

Let us believe in the God of Jesus Christ,
man among humankind,
who sings, laughs and cries,
who takes pleasure in music

and is deeply moved by a flower in bloom,
a God who is close, one of us, committed to us,
a God who walks with us,
and who in that journey
leads us beyond the path we would have taken
to other shores, to other lands.

   R. *Amen.*

The leader concludes by saying to those present:

May the Lord be with you always,
to be your strength and your peace.

   R. *Thanks be to God.*

World Day of the Sick

This observance is held on February 11, the feast of Our Lady of Lourdes. Arrange, if possible, to bring holy water blessed at Lourdes or another shrine of Our Lady with you.

Greeting

The leader offers a greeting to all present.

May the grace of our Lord Jesus Christ,
and the love of God,
and the fellowship of the Holy Spirit,
be with us all as we pray here together.
    R. Amen.

Gathering Prayer

The leader begins by saying this opening prayer.

O God, who has given us into the special care of the Blessed Virgin Mary, grant us the particular favors that we ask through her intercession. May we rejoice on her special feast day and look forward to the vision of her in heaven.
    R. Amen.

First Reading

The leader reads a passage from sacred Scripture. This text tells about God's healing power.

King Hezekiah fell ill and was at the point of death. The prophet Isaiah son of Amoz came and said to him, "The Lord says this, 'Put your affairs in order, for you are going to die, and you will not live.'" Hezekiah turned his face to the wall and addressed this prayer to the Lord, "Ah, Lord, remember I beg you how I have behaved faithful and with sincerity of heart in your presence and have done what is right in your eyes." And Hezekiah shed many tears.

Isaiah had not left the middle court, before the word of the Lord came to him, "Go back and say to Hezekiah, prince of my people, the Lord, the God of David your ancestor, says this: 'I have heard your prayer and seen your tears. I will cure you: in three days' time you shall go up to the Temple of the Lord. I will add fifteen years to your life. I will save you and this city from the hands of the king of Assyria, I will protect this city for my own sake and the sake of my servant David.'"

R. *Word of the Lord.*

Psalm 45:3

The leader prays a brief psalm.

You are the finest among all others,
your lips are anointed with graciousness,
for God has blessed you forever.

Our Father

The leader introduces the Lord's Prayer.

We commend all whom we love, or who have been entrusted to our prayers, to the unfailing love of God, and say together, as Christ himself has taught us:

R. *Our Father, who art in heaven,*
hallowed be thy name;
thy kingdom come;
thy will be done
on earth as it is in heaven.
Give us this day our daily bread,
and forgive us our trespasses,
as we forgive those who trespass
against us.
And lead us not into temptation,
but deliver us from evil.
Amen.

Second Reading

The leader reads this brief quotation.

We have the Blessed Virgin as our model—she has suffered much, she has loved to suffer to be more close to her Son, but she never complained. Not only did she not protest against the worries and complications of her life, which however difficult, left her heart free.

MOTHER MARIE DES DOULLEURS

Prayer for Comfort

The leader shares this prayer with those present.

Father, you are the unfailing refuge of those who suffer—bring peace and comfort to the sick and the infirm. Give all those who look after them knowledge, patience, and compassion. Inspire them with actions which will bring relief; words which will enlighten; and love which will bring comfort. We ask this through your son, Jesus Christ.

R. Amen.

Prayer for Pre-Surgery

Use this prayer where appropriate.

O God, you understand my feelings at this moment; you know my fears and my nervousness; you know the thoughts that I cannot put into words. I thank you for all the skill and wisdom of the surgeon, the anesthetist, and the nursing staff. Give them strength for their work today, and help me to place myself in their hands. I now place myself confidently in your loving hands, knowing that nothing can separate me from your love in Christ Jesus. I say, as long ago Jesus said, "Father, into your hands I commit myself. May your will be done."

R. Amen.

Let us remember in these prayers all who are sick and in need, our doctors, nurses, and caregivers, all our relatives and friends, living and dead, and the souls of all those recently deceased, as we seek the intercession of the Holy Mother of God, and say together:

R. Hail Mary, full of grace,
   the Lord is with thee.
   Blessed art thou among women
   and blessed is the fruit of thy womb Jesus.
   Holy Mary, Mother of God,
   pray for us sinners,
   now and at the hour of our death.
   Amen.

Prayer to Avoid Anxiety

After the assembly makes the sign of the cross, the leader says this prayer of Saint Francis de Sales.

Do not worry about what might happen tomorrow;
the same Everlasting Father who cares for you today
will take care of you tomorrow and every day.
Either he will shield you from suffering,
or he will give you unfailing strength to bear it.
So be at peace, then,
and put aside all anxious thoughts and imaginings.

The leader concludes by saying to those present:

May the Lord be with you always,
to be your strength and your peace.
   R. Thanks be to God.

Saint Joseph

This solemnity honoring the husband of the Blessed Virgin Mary and the patron of the Universal Church takes place on March 19.

Greeting

The leader offers a greeting to all present.

May the grace of our Lord Jesus Christ,
and the love of God,
and the fellowship of the Holy Spirit
be with us all as we pray here together.
    R. Amen.

Gathering Prayer

The leader begins by saying this opening prayer.

As Joseph has watched ever faithfully over your greatest gift to us, your Son, may he also watch over and guard us in our time of need.
    R. Amen.

First Reading

The leader reads a passage from sacred Scripture. This text tells about Joseph's role in Jesus' birth.

A reading from the Gospel according to
Matthew 1:18–25

This is how Jesus Christ came to be born. His mother Mary was betrothed to Joseph, but before they came to live together she was found to be with child through the Holy Spirit. Her husband Joseph, being a man of honor and wanting to spare her publicity, decided to divorce her informally.

He had made up his mind to do this when the angel of the Lord appeared to him in a dream and said, "Joseph, son of David, do not be afraid to take Mary home as your wife, because she has conceived what is in her by the Holy Spirit. She will give birth to a son and you must name him Jesus, because he is the one who is to save his people from their sins...."

When Joseph woke up, he did what the angel of the Lord had told him to do: he took his wife to his home and though he had not had intercourse with her, she gave birth to a son; and he named him Jesus.

R. *The Gospel of the Lord.*

Psalm 112:1–2

The leader prays a brief psalm.

Blessed is the one who fears the Lord,
who greatly delights in his commands.
His children will be powerful on earth;
the upright's offsprings will be blessed.

Our Father

The leader introduces the Lord's Prayer.

We commend all whom we love, or who have been entrusted to our prayers, to the unfailing love of God, and say together, as Christ himself has taught us:

> **R.** *Our Father, who art in heaven,*
> *hallowed be thy name;*
> *thy kingdom come;*
> *thy will be done*
> *on earth as it is in heaven.*
> *Give us this day our daily bread,*
> *and forgive us our trespasses*
> *as we forgive those who trespass*
> *against us,*
> *and lead us not into temptation,*
> *but deliver us from evil.*
> *Amen.*

Second Reading

The leader reads this brief quotation.

When Joseph [husband of Mary] does take up his assigned role, which in the view of the world still seems rather contemptible, he is handed an unexpected great gift: he is the one who gives the child the Messiah's name, something that he did not himself possess, not even as a descendant of David, yet something he is authorized to grant. We are dealing here with an essential aspect of God's single and integral plan of salvation. A complex web that has been spun for many centuries here receives its finishing touch from a man who has been specifically foreseen for the task....And it is good that Joseph adds not a single word of self-expression to the clear profile of his character in the story. The word that God speaks through Joseph needs none of that.

HANS URS VON BALTHASAR

Prayer to Alleviate Worry

The leader shares this prayer with those present.

Worry and pain, O Lord,
often make it difficult to pray.
Yet, Lord, we desire to pray,
to have communion with you,
to link to you those whom we love,
and those who have need of your love;
to thank you for those who look after us,
and those who wish us well.
O Lord, let us always remember
that to talk to you is prayer.

Lord Jesus,
we pray, that through our own troubles,
we may learn to understand the sufferings of others.
Help us to pass on to them
the compassion which you have given to us.
    R. *Amen.*

Let us remember in these prayers all who are sick and in need, our doctors, nurses, and caregivers, all our relatives and friends, living and dead, and the souls of all those recently deceased, as we seek the intercession of the Holy Mother of God, and say together:

R. *Hail Mary, full of grace,*
the Lord is with thee.
Blessed art thou among women
and blessed is the fruit of
thy womb Jesus.
Holy Mary, Mother of God,
pray for us sinners,
now and at the hour of our death.
Amen.

Prayer to Banish Worry

After the assembly makes the sign of the cross, the leader says this prayer.

Lord Jesus, I know I should not worry,
that worrying is bad for me;
but I cannot help it.
I worry about myself
and about what a burden I might be.

I worry about things
I cannot hope to change
and about little things that others might laugh at.
Help me to cast all my worries on you,
big and small, and to leave them with you.

Lord Jesus, I want
to accept help gratefully,
to take advice humbly,
but, more than anything, I want
to share everything with you
and to know your forgiving love.
    R. Amen.

The leader concludes by saying to those present:

May the Lord be with you always,
to be your strength and your peace.
    R. Thanks be to God.

Annunciation of the Lord

This solemn feast of March 25 commemorates the announcement by the archangel Gabriel to the Virgin Mary that she was to become the Mother of God.

Greeting

The leader offers a greeting to all present.

May the grace of our Lord Jesus Christ,
and the love of God,
and the fellowship of the Holy Spirit,
be with us all as we pray here together.
        R. Amen.

Gathering Prayer

The leader begins by saying this opening prayer.

O God, who sent an angel to convey the message of your Word-Made-Flesh in the womb of the Blessed Virgin Mary, grant that we her children also may be helped by her intercession with you.
        R. Amen.

First Reading

The leader reads a passage from sacred Scripture. This text recounts the Annunciation of the Lord to Mary.

A reading from the Gospel according to
Luke 1:26-38

In the sixth month the angel Gabriel was sent by God to a town in Galilee called Nazareth, to a virgin betrothed to a man named Joseph, of the house of David; and the virgin's name was Mary.

He went in and said to her, "Rejoice, so highly favored! The Lord is with you." She was deeply disturbed by these words, and asked herself what this greeting could mean, but the angel said to her, "Mary, do not be afraid; you have won God's favor. Listen! You are to conceive and bear a son, and you must name him Jesus. He will be great and will be called Son of the Most High. The Lord God will give him the throne of his ancestor David; he will rule over the House of Jacob for ever and his reign will have no end."

Mary said to the angel, "But how can this come about, since I am a virgin?"

"The Holy Spirit will come upon you," the angel answered, "and the power of the Most High will cover you with its shadow. And so the child will be holy and will be called Son of God. Know this too, your kinswoman Elizabeth has, in her old age, herself conceived a son, and she whom people called barren is now in her sixth month, *for nothing is impossible to God.*"

"I am the handmaid of the Lord," said Mary, "let what you have said be done to me." And the angel left her.

R. The Gospel of the Lord.

Psalm 45:11–14

The leader prays a brief psalm.

Listen, O daughter, pay attention;
forget your father's house and your nation,
and your beauty will charm the King....
The people of Tyre will bow before him.
The wealthiest nations will seek your favor.

Our Father

The leader introduces the Lord's Prayer.

We commend all whom we love, or who have been
entrusted to our prayers, to the unfailing love of God,
and say together, as Christ himself has taught us:

> **R.** *Our Father, who art in heaven,*
> *hallowed be thy name;*
> *thy kingdom come;*
> *thy will be done*
> *on earth as it is in heaven.*
> *Give us this day our daily bread,*
> *and forgive us our trespasses,*
> *as we forgive those who trespass*
> *against us,*
> *and lead us not into temptation,*
> *but deliver us from evil.*
> *Amen.*

Second Reading

The leader reads this brief quotation.

In what words did the angel break the happy news of Redemption? "Hail, thou that art full of grace, the Lord is with thee." The messenger of joy in his first word bids her to rejoice. He knew well that his message was of good tidings of great joy…to all creatures. …He knew well that it broke the power of corruption. He knew well that it brought victory over hell.…Therefore, when he began to speak, he spoke in tones of rejoicing. Therefore, he made the name of joy to herald the tidings of good, which were to be a joy unto all people.

Saint Sophronius

Prayer for the Afflicted

The leader shares this prayer with those present.

Dear Mary, our Mother,
we pray to your Son
for all the cares and anxieties
of those who have asked for our prayers:
Succor and restore the suffering in body and mind,
pity those who are tried by ill-health and disease,
give them light in darkness,
and in your great compassion,
lead them close to the strength of Jesus Christ,
your Son, our Lord.
   R. Amen.

Let us remember in these prayers all who are sick and in need, our doctors, nurses, and caregivers, our relatives and friends, living and dead, and the souls of all those recently deceased, as we seek the intercession of the Holy Mother of God, and say together:

> R. *Hail Mary, full of grace,*
> *the Lord is with thee.*
> *Blessed art thou among women*
> *and blessed is the fruit*
> *of thy womb Jesus.*
> *Holy Mary, Mother of God,*
> *pray for us sinners,*
> *now and at the hour of our death.*
> *Amen.*

Prayer for Those Who Are Lonely
After the assembly makes the sign of the cross, the leader says this prayer.

Dear Father in heaven, I am often alone
and it can be a time for dreaming,
for praying,
for catching up on things.
But I am thinking of those who are really alone,
alone in their loneliness,
alone even when surrounded by people;
desperately lonely, lonely in heart and in mind.
For those within our community who feel isolated,
Lord, let them know your healing love.

O beloved Lord,
whoever they may be, wherever they may be:
touch the sadness of their loneliness
with your presence.
Please hold them in your arms,
so that they may feel the sweet comfort
of your nearness,
and the depth of your everlasting love.
We ask this through Christ your Son.
R. Amen.

The leader concludes by saying to those present:

May the Lord be with you always,
to be your strength and your peace.
R. Thanks be to God.

Ash Wednesday

A movable observance that begins the penitential season of Lent—a period of forty days before Easter. Lent lasts until the Mass of the Lord's Supper on Holy Thursday.

Begin by asking those present to think for a moment of the first Station of the Cross: Mary sorrowing, hears the death sentence. "Crucify him, his blood be on us." Pray: "Mary, hear my prayer. Let the blood of Jesus be my redemption."

Greeting

The leader offers a greeting to all present.

May the grace of our Lord Jesus Christ,
and the love of God,
and the fellowship of the Holy Spirit,
be with us all as we pray here together.
      R. Amen.

Gathering Prayer

The leader begins by saying this opening prayer.

Lord, grant that we may successfully observe the works of Lent, prayer, fasting, and almsgiving. Let us reach out for the grace offered by your Son and, during this time, protect us from all evil, through our Lord Jesus Christ.
      R. Amen.

First Reading

The leader reads a passage from sacred Scripture. This text tells us that our day of salvation is at hand.

A reading from the Second Letter of Paul to the Corinthians 5:20–21, 6:1–2

We are Ambassadors for Christ; it is as though God were appealing through us, and the appeal that we make in Christ's name is: be reconciled to God. For our sake God made the sinless one into sin, so that in him we might become the goodness of God.

As his fellow workers, we beg you not to neglect the grace of God that you have received for he says: at the favorable time, I have listened to you; on the day of salvation I came to your help.

Well, now is the favorable time; this is the day of salvation.

R. The Word of the Lord.

Psalm 51:3–4, 10–11

The leader prays a brief psalm.

Have mercy on me, O God, in your love.
In your great compassion blot out my sin.
Wash me thoroughly of my guilt;
cleanse me of evil....

Fill me with joy and gladness;
let the bones you have crushed rejoice.
Turn your face away from my sins
and blot out all my offenses.

Our Father

The leader introduces the Lord's Prayer.

We commend all whom we love, or who have been entrusted to our prayers, to the unfailing love of God, and say together, as Christ himself has taught us:

> *R. Our Father, who art in heaven,*
> *hallowed be thy name;*
> *thy kingdom come;*
> *thy will be done on earth as it is in heaven.*
> *Give us this day our daily bread,*
> *and forgive us our trespasses,*
> *as we forgive those who trespass*
> *against us,*
> *and lead us not into temptation,*
> *but deliver us from evil.*
> *Amen.*

Second Reading

The leader reads this brief quotation.

The presence of God is the soul's life and nourishment, which can be acquired by the Lord's grace. Here are the means: a great purity of life, keeping constant

guard not to do, say, or think anything that might dis-
please God; and when something like that happens, to
humbly ask him pardon and do penance for it; a great
fidelity to the practice of this presence and to the fos-
tering of this awareness of God within must always be
carried out gently, humbly, and lovingly.

BROTHER LAWRENCE, *PRACTICE OF THE PRESENCE OF GOD*

Prayer for Repentance

The leader shares this prayer with those present.

Lord, give us the grace to keep Lent faithfully,
and protect us in our struggle against evil.
As we begin the discipline of Lent,
make this season holy
by our continued suffering and self-denial.
Father in heaven,
the light of your truth bestows sight
to the darkness of sinful eyes.
May this season of repentance
bring us the blessing of your forgiveness
and the gift of your light.
We ask this through our Lord Jesus Christ.
   R. Amen.

Let us remember in these prayers all who are sick
and in need, our doctors, the nurses, and caregivers,
our relatives and friends, living and dead, and the souls
of all those recently deceased, as we seek the intercession of the Holy Mother of God, and say together:

R. *Hail Mary, full of grace,*
the Lord is with thee.
Blessed art thou among women
and blessed is the fruit of thy womb Jesus.
Holy Mary, Mother of God,
pray for us sinners,
now and at the hour of our death.
Amen.

Prayer for Serenity

Making the sign of the cross, the leader says this prayer.

Father, you do not protect us against catastrophes,
but in them you come to our aid.
It is in the very midst of tempest and misfortune
that a wonderful zone of peace, serenity, and joy
bursts in on us if we dwell in your grace.

You do not help us
before we have helped ourselves,
but when we are at the end of our resources,
you manifest yourself, and we begin to know
that you have been there all the time.
We thank you, through Christ our Lord.
R. *Amen.*

The leader concludes by saying to those present:

May the Lord be with you always,
to be your strength and your peace.
R. *Thanks be to God.*

Lent Week 1

In preparation, recall Christ's wounded shoulder from the second Station of the Cross. Mary sees the precious blood flow from the wounded shoulder. "O Mary, help us to shoulder our cross patiently, in union with Jesus."

Greeting

The leader offers a greeting to all present.

May the grace of our Lord Jesus Christ,
and the love of God,
and the fellowship of the Holy Spirit,
be with us all as we pray here together.
   R. Amen.

Gathering Prayer

The leader begins by saying this opening prayer.

   O God, help us to put aside any suggestion of evil so that we may follow our Lord in his vanquishing of temptation. If we fail, bring us back from evil and heal us in our repentance.
   R. Amen.

First Reading

The leader reads a passage from sacred Scripture. The theme of this text is endurance.

Remember all the sufferings that you had to meet after you received the light, in earlier days; sometimes by being yourselves publicly exposed to insults and violence, and sometimes as associates of others who were treated in the same way. For you not only shared in the sufferings of those who were in prison, but you happily accepted being stripped of your belongings, knowing that you owned something that was better and lasting. Be as confident now, then, since the reward is so great.

You will need endurance to do God's will and gain what he has promised.

R. The Word of the Lord.

Psalm 91:9–12

The leader prays a brief psalm.

If you have made the Lord your refuge,
the Most High your stronghold,
no harm will come upon you,
no disaster will draw near your home.
For he will command his angels
to guard you in all your ways.
They will lift you up with their hands
so that your foot will not hit a stone.

Our Father

The leader introduces the Lord's Prayer.

We commend all whom we love, or who have been entrusted to our prayers, to the unfailing love of God, and say together, as Christ himself has taught us:

R. *Our Father, who art in heaven,*
   hallowed be thy name;
   thy kingdom come;
   thy will be done
   on earth as it is in heaven.
   Give us this day our daily bread,
   and forgive us our trespasses,
   as we forgive those who trespass
   against us,
   and lead us not into temptation,
   but deliver us from evil.
   Amen.

Second Reading

The leader reads this brief quotation.

Whenever, for love of me, you willingly submit to the calamities which other men cause you; accept with lamblike meekness and silence the violent rage of all men; are indifferent as to the instigators of the plot against you, its violence, and whether you are in the right or in the wrong; and by your gentle spirit, meek words, and gracious demeanor conquer the malice of

your adversaries: behold, then the true representation
of my death is effected in you....

BLESSED HENRY SUSO

Prayer for Strength

The leader shares this prayer with those present.

Lord, help those in pain, suffering, and illness
to know that the father cares for them
for He loves them as He loves his own son Jesus.
Lord your servant Paul said,
"When I am weak, then I am strong."
We feel so weak,
pray God that we may be strong.
Father of love, hear our prayers.
Help us to know your will,
and to do it with courage and faith.
We ask this through your son, Jesus Christ.
   R. Amen.

Let us remember in these prayers all who are sick
and in need, our doctors, nurses, and caregivers, all our
relatives and friends, living and dead, and the souls of
all those recently deceased, as we seek the intercession
of the Holy Mother of God, and say together:

R. Hail Mary, full of grace,
   the Lord is with thee.
   Blessed art thou among women
   and blessed is the fruit
   of thy womb Jesus.

Holy Mary, Mother of God,
pray for us sinners,
now and at the hour of our death.
Amen.

Prayer for Salvation

After the assembly makes the sign of the cross, the leader says this prayer.

Lord, may this Lenten undertaking,
free us from our old life of sin,
and make us your new creation.
Help us to be pilgrims,
on the way that leads to eternal life,
and be with us now and always.
We ask this through Christ our Lord.
    R. Amen.

The leader concludes by saying to those present:

May the Lord be with you always,
to be your strength and your peace.
    R. Thanks be to God.

Lent Week 2

In preparation, let us recall the seventh Station of the Cross, wherein Jesus falls the second time. With every step, the path becomes harder, the burden heavier, and more crushing for Christ. Lord, in my weakness, be my strength.

Greeting

The leader offers a greeting to all present.

May the grace of our Lord Jesus Christ,
and the love of God,
and the fellowship of the Holy Spirit,
be with us all as we pray here together.
    R. Amen.

Gathering Prayer

The leader begins by saying this opening prayer.

    Look down upon us, O Lord, and grant that the sufferings of our bodies and minds may be transformed into the chastening of our souls, and our defense from all evil.
    R. Amen.

First Reading

The leader reads a passage from sacred Scripture. This text recalls Christ's words about the holy Eucharist.

A reading from the Gospel according to
John 6:54–58

Anyone who eats my flesh and drinks my blood
has eternal life,
And I shall raise him up on the last day.
For my flesh is real food
and my blood is real drink.
He who eats my flesh and drinks my blood
lives in me
and I live in him.
As I, who am sent by the living Father,
myself draw life from the Father,
so whoever eats me will draw life from me.
This is the bread come down from heaven;
and anyone who eats this bread will live for ever.

    R. *The Gospel of the Lord.*

Psalm 25:17–20

The leader prays a brief psalm.

Free my heart of bitterness;
relieve me of this distress.
See my pain and sufferings,
and forgive all my sins.
See how my enemies have increased
and how violently they hate me.
Deliver me from them;
let me not be put to shame.

Our Father

The leader introduces the Lord's Prayer.

We commend all whom we love, or who have been entrusted to our prayers, to the unfailing love of God, and say together, as Christ himself has taught us:

> **R.** *Our Father, who art in heaven,*
> *hallowed be thy name;*
> *thy kingdom come;*
> *thy will be done*
> *on earth as it is in heaven.*
> *Give us this day our daily bread,*
> *and forgive us our trespasses,*
> *as we forgive those who trespass*
> *against us,*
> *and lead us not into temptation,*
> *but deliver us from evil.*
> *Amen.*

Second Reading

The leader reads this brief quotation.

We know that the Holy Spirit will come to us only when we are poor and weak, when we appear before Jesus and say, "Here I am, confused and poor; here I am with all my sins, with all my barriers and difficulties; you alone are my Savior, I believe in you, and I believe that you are ready to act precisely at this moment when we are in greatest need, in the greatest confusion, or when we are in the greatest moment of sadness and anguish?"

JEAN VANIER

Prayer of Request

The leader shares this prayer with those present.

Merciful Father, take away all our offenses and sins;
purify us in body and soul,
remit our sins,
wash away our guilt,
help us to end our evil thoughts,
and aid us in the rebirth of our better instincts.
May we do works pleasing to you
and profitable to our health in body and soul.
We ask this through Christ our Lord.
    R. Amen.

Let us remember in these prayers all who are sick
and in need, and also the doctors, the nurses, the
caregivers, all our relatives and friends, living and dead,
and the souls of all those recently deceased, as we seek
the intercession of the Holy Mother of God, and say
together:

> *R. Hail Mary, full of grace,*
> *the Lord is with thee.*
> *Blessed art thou among women*
> *and blessed is the fruit*
> *of thy womb Jesus.*

Holy Mary, Mother of God,
pray for us sinners,
now and at the hour of our death.
Amen.

Prayer for Faithfulness

Those assembled make the sign of the cross, and the leader says this prayer.

All-powerful God,
Help us to thank you by lives of faithful service.
May we find through you a lasting remedy
for body and soul.
We ask this through Christ our Lord.
    R. *Amen.*

The leader concludes by saying to those present:

May the Lord be with you always,
to be your strength and your peace.
    R. *Thanks be to God.*

Lent Week 3

In preparation, let us recall the ninth Station of the Cross wherein Jesus falls the third time. Recall that "Thrice he falls by lashes torn, in his blood I rise reborn."

Greeting

The leader offers a greeting to all present.

May the grace of our Lord Jesus Christ,
and the love of God,
and the fellowship of the Holy Spirit,
be with us all as we pray here together.
    R. *Amen.*

Gathering Prayer

The leader begins by saying this opening prayer.

God, our Father, we human beings are fragile creatures even if we carry the mark of baptism. Strengthen us with your Word. Through Jesus Christ our Lord.
    R. *Amen.*

First Reading

The leader reads a passage from sacred Scripture. This text tells about humility and its outcome—peace.

A reading from the Letter of James 3:13–18

If there are any wise or learned men among you, let them show it by their good lives, with humility and wisdom in their actions. But if at heart you have the bitterness of jealousy, or a self-seeking ambition, never make any claims for yourself or cover up the truth with lies—principles of this kind are not the wisdom that comes down from above: they are only earthly, animal and devilish. Wherever you find jealousy and ambition, you find disharmony, and wicked things of every kind being done; whereas the wisdom that comes down from above is essentially something pure; it also makes for peace, and is kindly and considerate; it is full of compassion and shows itself by doing good; nor is there any trace of partiality or hypocrisy in it. Peacemakers, when they work for peace, sow the seeds which will bear fruit in holiness.

R. *The Word of the Lord.*

Psalm 19:8–9

The leader prays a brief psalm.

The law of the Lord is perfect:
it gives life to the soul.
The word of the Lord is trustworthy:
it gives wisdom to the simple.
The precepts of the Lord are right;
they give joy to the heart.
The commandments of the Lord are clear:
they enlighten the eyes.

Our Father

The leader introduces the Lord's Prayer.

We commend all whom we love, or who have been entrusted to our prayers, to the unfailing love of God, and say together, as Christ himself has taught us:

R. *Our Father, who art in heaven,*
   hallowed be thy name;
   thy kingdom come;
   thy will be done
   on earth as it is in heaven.
   Give us this day our daily bread,
   and forgive us our trespasses
   as we forgive those who trespass against us,
   and lead us not into temptation,
   but deliver us from evil.
   Amen.

Second Reading

The leader reads this brief quotation.

We return again and again to the same petty, boring, everyday sins: irritability, despondency, gloom, envy, vanity and malice conquer us in the same old way. Who will lead us out of this blind alley? Who can pull us out of the swamp in which our souls are stuck fast and perishing? We have no help or salvation other than the Lord Jesus Christ and his love—his extra love.

ALEXANDER MEN

Prayer for Peace

The leader shares this prayer with those present.

Father in Heaven, creator of all,
look down on your people
in their moments of need,
for you alone are the source of our peace.
Bring us to the dignity
which distinguishes the poor in spirit
and show us how great is the call to serve,
that we may share in the peace of Christ,
who offered his life in the service of all.
We ask this through your son, Jesus Christ.
  R. Amen.

Let us remember in these prayers all who are sick and in need, our doctors, nurses, and caregivers, all our relatives and friends, living and dead, and the souls of all those recently deceased, as we seek the intercession of the Holy Mother of God, and say together:

  R. Hail Mary, full of grace,
  the Lord is with thee,
  Blessed art thou among women
  and blessed is the fruit
  of thy womb Jesus.
  Holy Mary, Mother of God,
  pray for us sinners,
  now and at the hour of our death.
  Amen.

Prayer for Renewal of Faith

Those assembled make the sign of the cross, and the leader says this prayer.

Heavenly Father,
send the Holy Spirit upon your Church,
to renew us in faith.
Enable us to share the good news of the Gospel
in word and in deed—
so that men and women may be drawn to your love,
and follow the way of your Son, Jesus,
who is the Way, the Truth, and the Life.
We make our prayer through Christ our Lord.
    R. Amen.

The leader concludes by saying to those present:

May the Lord be with you always,
to be your strength and your peace.
    R. Thanks be to God.

Lent Week 4

We now recall the tenth Station of the Cross: Jesus is stripped of his garments. We feel the humiliation and pain, the absence of all dignity. Lord, may we remember that it is not what we have, but how you see us, that gives us all our deepest dignity.

Greeting

The leader offers a greeting to all present.

May the grace of our Lord Jesus Christ,
and the love of God,
and the fellowship of the Holy Spirit,
be with us all as we pray here together.
  R. Amen.

Gathering Prayer

The leader begins by saying this opening prayer.

  Grant, O Lord, that we may be consoled by your grace, even as we suffer justly for our sins.
  R. Amen.

First Reading

The leader reads a passage from sacred Scripture. The theme of this text is sure salvation through Christ's cross.

A reading from the First Letter of Paul to the Corinthians 1:18–25

The language of the cross may be illogical to those who are not on the way to salvation, but those of us who are on the way see it as God's power to save. As scripture says: *I shall destroy the wisdom of the wise and bring to nothing all the learning of the learned. Where are the philosophers now? Where are the scribes?* Where are any of our thinkers today? Do you see now how God has shown up the foolishness of human wisdom? If it was God's wisdom that human wisdom should not know God, it was because God wanted to save those who have faith through the foolishness of the message that we preach. And so, while the Jews demand miracles and the Greeks look for wisdom, here are we preaching a crucified Christ. To the Jews an obstacle that they cannot get over—to the pagans madness, but to those who have been called, whether they are Jews or Greeks, a Christ who is the power and the wisdom of God. For God's foolishness is wiser than human wisdom, and God's weakness is stronger than human strength.

R. The Word of the Lord.

Psalm 126:3–5

The leader prays a brief psalm.

The Lord had done great things for us,
and we were glad indeed.
Bring back our exiles, O Lord,

like fresh streams in the desert.
Those who sow in tears
will leap with songs and shouts of joy.

Our Father

The leader introduces the Lord's Prayer.

We commend all whom we love, or who have been entrusted to our prayers, to the unfailing love of God, and say together, as Christ himself has taught us:

> *R. Our Father, who art in heaven,*
> *hallowed be thy name;*
> *thy kingdom come;*
> *thy will be done*
> *on earth as it is in heaven.*
> *Give us this day our daily bread,*
> *and forgive us our trespasses*
> *as we forgive those who trespass*
> *against us,*
> *and lead us not into temptation,*
> *but deliver us from evil.*
> *Amen.*

Second Reading

The leader reads this brief quotation.

Let those who want Christ to spare them have compassion for the poor. Let those who desire a bond with the fellowship of the blessed be readily disposed toward nourishing the wretched. No human being should be considered worthless by another. That nature which the Creator of the universe made his own should not be looked down upon in anyone….Your fellow servant receives assistance, and the Lord returns thanks. Food for someone in need is the cost of purchasing the kingdom of heaven, and the one who is generous with temporal things is made heir of the eternal.

POPE LEO THE GREAT

Prayer for Lost Souls

The leader shares this prayer with those present.

Let us pray,
for all who die and are not mourned,
but are ignored in death
like a stone on the wayside.

Let us pray,
for all who are lost in war and prison,
for those who have committed suicide,
and those who are lonely in life and death,
that God may hear them
and keep them in his heart.
Lord hear our prayer,
through Christ your Son.
   R. Amen.

Let us remember in these prayers all who are sick and in need, our doctors, nurses, and caregivers, all our relatives and friends, living and dead, and the souls of all those recently deceased, as we seek the intercession of the Holy Mother of God, and say together:

R. Hail Mary, full of grace,
the Lord is with thee.
Blessed art thou among women
and blessed is the fruit of thy womb Jesus.
Holy Mary, Mother of God,
pray for us sinners,
now and at the hour of our death.
Amen.

Prayer for Wisdom

Making the sign of the cross, the leader says this prayer.

Father,
you give us food from heaven.
By our sharing in this mystery,
teach us to judge wisely the things of earth
and to love the things of heaven.
Grant this through Christ our Lord.
R. Amen.

The leader concludes by saying to those present:

May the Lord be with you always,
to be your strength and your peace.
R. Thanks be to God.

Lent Week 5

In this final week of Lent, we recall the thirteenth Station of the Cross: Jesus is brought down from the cross. Let us ask Mary that as she takes her son from the cross, may she take us too when life is done.

Greeting

The leader offers a greeting to all present.

May the grace of our Lord Jesus Christ,
and the love of God,
and the fellowship of the Holy Spirit,
be with us all as we pray here together.
    R. Amen.

Gathering Prayer

The leader begins by saying this opening prayer.

    Draw near to us, O Lord our God, and with your perpetual help which we hope never to underestimate keep us from the death of sin. Rather, keep us always in the light of your mercy.
    R. Amen.

First Reading

The leader reads a passage from sacred Scripture. This text tells about the great mercy of God.

A reading from the prophet Isaiah 25:6–9

On this mountain,
the Lord of hosts will prepare for all peoples
a banquet of rich food, a banquet of fine wines.
On this mountain he will remove
the mourning veil covering all peoples,
and the shroud enwrapping all nations.
He will destroy Death for ever.
The Lord will wipe away
the tears from every cheek;
    he will take away his people's shame
        everywhere on earth,
           for the Lord has said so.
That day, it will be said: See, this is our God
    in whom we hoped for salvation;
        the Lord is the one in whom we hoped.
We exult and we rejoice
that he has saved us.
    R. The Word of the Lord.

Psalm 119:25, 28–29

The leader prays a brief psalm.

In the dust I lie prostrate;
lift me up, as promised by your word....
My soul is weary with sorrow;
strengthen me according to your word.
Keep me away from deceitful paths;
be gracious and teach me your law.

Our Father

The leader introduces the Lord's Prayer.

We commend all whom we love, or who have been entrusted to our prayers, to the unfailing love of God, and say together, as Christ himself has taught us:

> **R.** *Our Father, who art in heaven,*
> *hallowed be thy name;*
> *thy kingdom come;*
> *thy will be done*
> *on earth as it is in heaven.*
> *Give us this day our daily bread,*
> *and forgive us our trespasses,*
> *as we forgive those who trespass*
> *against us,*
> *and lead us not into temptation,*
> *but deliver us from evil.*
> *Amen.*

Second Reading

The leader reads this brief quotation.

When, in your troubles, you have been unable to supply the appropriate remedy, God requires that you should remain in a state of abandonment to his good pleasure, awaiting from his goodness the help you need, after the example of those who waited patiently for him to supply their wants without even troubling to expose them. You may, in fact, rest assured that God will not allow you to be tried beyond your strength. It is when human beings are powerless that he does all, and thereby manifests his power and goodness.

SAINT JOHN BAPTIST DE LA SALLE

Prayer for Strength for the Weary

The leader shares this prayer with those present.

When I am strong I will fight,
and when I am weary of the fight I will rest in you,
knowing that you can carry me for a time.
In my fight, I will draw strength from your love,
for your love cannot be beaten.

When I am alone,
when I meet the icy touch of fear,
I will take it in my hand and hold it out to you
and the heat of your love will melt it away.

When my heart feels isolated,
when no one can comfort me,
and the crowd serves only to remind me
    of how alone I am,
I will look within myself to where you wait,
and I will remember to allow you to love me.

Then, when the joy is so strong
that I cannot absorb life quickly enough,
I will remember to take a moment to sit with you,
and appreciate the beauty you created.

And when the night comes,
I ask only that I be alive with peace and faith,
so that I may not fear the new day that lies beyond.
> R. Amen.

Let us remember in these prayers all who are sick
and in need, our doctors, nurses, and caregivers, all our
relatives and friends, living and dead, and the souls of
all those recently deceased, as we seek the intercession
of the Holy Mother of God, and say together:

> R. Hail Mary, full of grace,
> the Lord is with thee.
> Blessed art thou among women
> and blessed is the fruit
> of thy womb Jesus.
> Holy Mary, Mother of God,
> pray for us sinners,
> now and at the hour of our death.
> Amen.

Prayer for Forgiveness

*Those assembled make the sign of the cross, and the leader
says this final prayer.*

Let us believe in the God of Jesus Christ
who welcomes sinners
and loves to forgive,
for we only rescue what we love.

God so loved the world
that God gave an only Son
to show that love.
Because God is love
the person who doesn't love
isn't really alive.
    R. Amen.

The leader concludes by saying to those present:

May the Lord be with you always,
to be your strength and your peace.
    R. Thanks be to God.

Passion Sunday or Palm Sunday

The Sunday before Easter marks the start of Holy Week and recalls the entry of Christ into Jerusalem at the beginning of the last week of his life on earth. This observance includes the blessing of palms.

Greeting

The leader offers a greeting to all present.

May the grace of our Lord Jesus Christ,
and the love of God,
and the fellowship of the Holy Spirit,
be with us all as we pray here together.
>   *R. Amen.*

Gathering Prayer

The leader begins by saying this opening prayer.

>   Almighty and Eternal God, who gave us an example of true humility in the person of your Son, our Lord, Jesus Christ, grant that we may be worthy of the heritage of his suffering on the cross.
>   *R. Amen.*

First Reading

The leader reads a passage from sacred Scripture. This text tells about the Good News of our salvation.

A reading according to the Gospel of Luke 4:16–21

Jesus came to Nazareth, where he had been brought up, and went into the synagogue on the Sabbath day as he usually did. He stood up to read, and they handed him the scroll of the prophet Isaiah. Unrolling the scroll he found the place where it is written:

The spirit of the Lord has been given to me,
for he has anointed me.
He has sent me to bring the good news to the poor,
to proclaim liberty to captives
and to the blind new sight,
to set the downtrodden free,
to proclaim the Lord's year of favor.

He then rolled up the scroll, gave it back to the assistant and sat down. And all eyes in the synagogue were fixed on him. Then he began to speak to them, "This text is being fulfilled today even as you listen."
R. The Gospel of the Lord.

Psalm 22:18–20

The leader prays a brief psalm.

They can count all my bones,
for they are looking and watching me,
dividing my garments among them
and casting lots for my raiment.
O Lord, be not far from me!

Our Father

The leader introduces the Lord's Prayer.

We commend all whom we love, or who have been entrusted to our prayers, to the unfailing love of God, and say together, as Christ himself has taught us:

R. *Our Father, who art in heaven,*
hallowed be thy name;
thy kingdom come;
thy will be done on earth as it is in heaven.
Give us this day our daily bread,
and forgive us our trespasses
as we forgive those who trespass against us,
and lead us not into temptation,
but deliver us from evil.
Amen.

Second Reading

The leader reads this brief quotation.

When I am sad, discouraged about myself and about others, I must think of Jesus in his glory, sitting on the right hand of the Father forever, and rejoice. I should at these times say the glorious mysteries of the rosary, so as to bathe my spirit in joy. Our Lord speaks, "Never worry about small things. Break away from all that is small and mean, and try to live on the heights, not from pride, but from love."

CHARLES DE FOUCAULD

Prayer of Contemplation on the Cross

The leader shares this prayer with those present. This prayer has been adapted for use in the presence of those who are disabled.

To help us to be closer to God as we approach Holy Week let us focus on the most familiar sign of a Christian—the cross. This will help us to recall the Trinity, and also the passion and death of Christ. So try to relax and ask the Holy Spirit to help you feel more comfortable.

Those of you able to see well enough—you can either focus on this crucifix on the table before us, or simply close your eyes and contemplate.

For any of you unable to focus on that distance, just close your eyes—try to relax and let the Holy Spirit who is now with us take over.

Now we all relax in the presence of God, and think deeply of the cross, think as deeply as you can.

First, we try to raise our mind and thoughts upwards, contemplating the head of Jesus crowned with thorns, upwards in adoration to God the Father. Next, we look downwards to the foot of the cross, in sorrow for refusing his love.

Now look towards the left, along the crossbeam of the cross at your past life. Thank God for it, the downs as well as the ups, and as our mind travels slowly across from left to right, we thank God for his continuous presence here today at this service, and every day through the loving care we receive.

Last, let us now move our minds to the right, along the crossbeam towards the future, and whatever the Father's plan for each of us may hold.

As we come slowly out of this quiet and peaceful prayer, let us now, with our minds, or perhaps with our hands, make the sign of the cross: "In the name of the Father...

(Pause for reflection)

Let us remember in these prayers all who are sick and in need, our doctors, nurses, and caregivers, all our relatives and friends, living and dead, and the souls of all those recently deceased, as we seek the intercession of the Holy Mother of God, and say together:

> **R.** *Hail Mary, full of grace,*
> *the Lord is with thee.*
> *Blessed art thou among women*
> *and blessed is the fruit*
> *of thy womb Jesus.*
> *Holy Mary, Mother of God,*
> *pray for us sinners,*
> *now and at the hour of our death.*
> *Amen.*

Prayer for Understanding

Those assembled make the sign of the cross, and the leader says this prayer.

My Lord, Jesus Christ,
you are the Light of the world.
I implore you to enlighten me,
and to disperse the darkness of my soul.
Give me true faith, firm hope, and perfect love.
Help me, O Lord, to come to know you so well,
that in all things I may act by your light,
and in accordance with your holy will.
You are the Way that leads to life.
    R. Amen.

The leader concludes by saying to those present:

May the Lord be with you always,
to be your strength and your peace.
    R. Thanks be to God.

Easter Sunday

A movable celebration commemorating the Resurrection of Christ. Its observance is determined by the first full moon following the vernal equinox (between March 22 and April 25).

Greeting

The leader offers a greeting to all present.

May the grace of our Lord Jesus Christ,
and the love of God,
and the fellowship of the Holy Spirit,
be with us all as we pray here together.
> R. Amen.

Gathering Prayer

The leader begins by saying this opening prayer.

Heavenly Father, we offer all our hopes and petitions to you on this feast of your risen Son. May we banish all sorrow and joyfully celebrate Christ's Resurrection.
> R. Amen.

First Reading

The leader reads a passage from sacred Scripture. The theme of this text is Christ's glorious Resurrection.

You have been taught that when we were baptized in Christ Jesus we were baptized in his death; in other words, when we were baptized we went into the tomb with him and joined him in death, so that as Christ was raised from the dead by the Father's glory, we too might live a new life.

If in union with Christ we have imitated his death, we shall also imitate him in the resurrection. We must realize that our former selves have been crucified with him to destroy this sinful body and to free us from the slavery of sin. When a man dies, of course, he has finished with sin.

But we believe that having died with Christ we shall return to life with him; Christ, as we know, having been raised from the dead will never die again. Death has no power over him any more.

When he died, he died, once for all, to sin, so his life now is life with God; and in that way, you too must consider yourselves to be dead to sin, but alive to God in Christ Jesus.

R. *The Word of the Lord.*

Psalm 118:17–18

The leader prays a brief psalm.

I shall not die, but live
to proclaim what the Lord has done.
The Lord has stricken me severely,
but he has saved me from death.

Our Father

The leader introduces the Lord's Prayer.

We commend all whom we love, or who have been entrusted to our prayers, to the unfailing love of God, and say together, as Christ himself has taught us:

R. Our Father, who art in heaven,
hallowed be thy name;
thy kingdom come;
thy will be done
on earth as it is in heaven.
Give us this day our daily bread,
and forgive us our trespasses
as we forgive those who trespass
against us,
and lead us not into temptation,
but deliver us from evil.
Amen.

Second Reading

The leader reads this brief quotation.

Animals are interested only in eating, drinking, and sleeping. The same may be said of those who take more care of their bodies than of the soul, who love their stomachs and senses better that chastity and justice. You must know that we are Christians precisely in order that we may remember heaven and eternal happiness, and may think more of our souls than of our bodies. Our body will last only a few years in this world; our soul, on the contrary, if it be good, shall live forever in heaven.

SAINT BONIFACE

Prayer of Joy in the Resurrection

The leader shares this prayer with those present.

Father,
in the rising of your Son,
death gives birth to new life.
The sufferings he endured
have restored hope to a fallen world.
Let sin never ensnare us
with empty promises of passing joy.
Make us one with you always,
so that our joy may be holy,
and our love may give life.
We ask this through Christ our Lord.
    R. Amen.

Let us remember in these prayers all who are sick and in need, our doctors, nurses, and caregivers, all our relatives and friends, living and dead, and the souls of all those recently deceased, as we seek the intercession of the Holy Mother of God, and say together:

R. *Hail Mary, full of grace,*
the Lord is with thee.
Blessed art thou among women
and blessed is the fruit
of thy womb Jesus.
Holy Mary, Mother of God,
pray for us sinners,
now and at the hour of our death.
Amen.

Prayer of New Life in Christ

Those assembled make the sign of the cross, and the leader says this final prayer.

Lord Jesus Christ,
during this Easter Season,
may your Holy Spirit deepen our awareness
of the mystery of salvation.
In baptism we died to sin
and accepted your grace;
help us now to experience the joy
of the resurrection in our own lives.
May our forgiveness and loving service of others
be signs of the new life we have received.

And may our faith, hope, and love
be strengthened day by day
throughout our entire lives.
This we pray in your name, our Risen Lord.
   R. Amen. Alleluia!

The leader concludes by saying to those present:

May the Lord be with you always,
to be your strength and your peace.
   R. Thanks be to God.

Easter Week 2

Greeting

The leader offers a greeting to all present.

May the grace of our Lord Jesus Christ,
and the love of God,
and the fellowship of the Holy Spirit,
be with us all as we pray here together.
    R. Amen.

Gathering Prayer

The leader begins by saying this opening prayer.

Give our hearts gladness, O God, in the knowledge that Easter is the working out of our salvation. We are grateful for the gift of our redemption.
    R. Amen.

First Reading

The leader reads a passage from sacred Scripture. The theme of this text is trust in God.

A reading from the Gospel according to John 14:1–7

Jesus said to his disciples:
"Do not let your hearts be troubled.
Trust in God still, and trust in me.

There are many rooms in my Father's house;
if there were not, I should have told you.
I am going now to prepare a place for you,
and after I have gone and prepared you a place,
I shall return to take you with me;
so that where I am, you may be too.
You know the way to the place where I am going."

Thomas said, "Lord, we do not know where you are going. so how can we know the way?" Jesus said: "I am the Way, the Truth, and the Life. No one can come to the Father except through me."

R. The Gospel of the Lord.

Psalm 118:24–26

The leader prays a brief psalm.

This is the day the Lord has made;
so let us rejoice and be glad.
Save us, O Lord, deliver us, O Lord!
Blessed is he who comes in the Lord's name!

Our Father

The leader introduces the Lord's Prayer.

We commend all whom we love, or who have been entrusted to our prayers, to the unfailing love of God, and say together, as Christ himself has taught us:

R. *Our Father, who art in heaven,*
hallowed be thy name;
thy kingdom come;
thy will be done
on earth as it is in heaven.
Give us this day our daily bread,
and forgive us our trespasses,
as we forgive those who trespass
against us,
and lead us not into temptation,
but deliver us from evil.
Amen.

Second Reading

The leader reads this brief quotation.

It is not enough that we suffer with Christ, we must also persevere in our sufferings: for only "he that shall persevere unto the end shall be saved." The end is the test, and praise is sung only at the going out. But in order to persevere, let each one in all humility pray to God for help, for "it is not of him who runs, but of God who shows mercy." The mercy of God is better than life, however great a boon life may be to human beings. But they are not worthy of mercy who do not acknowledge their wretchedness in the sight of God, nor feel that they can be rescued from the many dangers surrounding them only by the mercy of God.

SAINT COLUMBAN

Prayer to Obtain the Treasures of Heaven

The leader shares this prayer with those present.

Father, watch over your family
and keep us safe in your care,
for all our hope is in you.

In faith and love we ask you, Father,
to watch over your family gathered here.
In your mercy and loving kindness,
no thought of ours is left unguarded,
no tear unheeded, no joy unnoticed.

Through the prayers of Jesus,
may the blessings promised to the poor in spirit
lead us to the treasures of your heavenly kingdom.
> *R. Amen.*

Let us remember in these prayers all who are sick
and in need, our doctors, nurses, and caregivers, all our
relatives and friends, living and dead, and the souls of
all those recently deceased, as we seek the intercession
of the Holy Mother of God, and say together:

> *R. Hail Mary, full of grace,*
> *the Lord is with thee.*
> *Blessed art thou among women*
> *and blessed is the fruit of thy womb Jesus.*
> *Holy Mary, Mother of God,*
> *pray for us sinners,*
> *now and at the hour of our death.*
> *Amen.*

Prayer for Faith in God

Those assembled make the sign of the cross, and the leader says this prayer.

Let us believe in the God of Jesus Christ
who changes how things are,
who enters human life,
who is born, who suffers, who dies:
to save the world, to free us.
who gives us a taste for life
and who makes us responsible for our lives
personally and collectively.
    R. Amen.

The leader concludes by saying to those present:

May the Lord be with you always,
to be your strength and your peace.
    R. Thanks be to God.

Easter Week 3

Greeting

The leader offers a greeting to all present.

May the grace of our Lord Jesus Christ,
and the love of God,
and the fellowship of the Holy Spirit,
be with us all as we pray here together.
    R. *Amen.*

Gathering Prayer

The leader begins by saying this opening prayer.

Dear Lord, keep us from straying from the path of your justice, and always let us wear the white mantle of one who is committed to you always.
    R. *Amen.*

First Reading

The leader reads a passage from sacred Scripture. The theme of this text is salvation for all peoples.

A reading from the Acts of the Apostles 13:44–52

The next Sabbath almost the whole town of Antioch assembled to hear the word of God. When they saw the crowds, the Jews, prompted by jealousy, used blasphemies and contradicted everything that Paul had said. Then Paul and Barnabas spoke out boldly: "We had to proclaim the word of God to you first, but since you have rejected it, since you do not think yourselves worthy of eternal life, we must turn to the pagans. For this is what the Lord commanded us to do when he said: 'I have made you a light for the nations, so that my salvation may reach the ends of the earth.'"

It made the pagans very happy to hear this and they thanked the Lord for his message; all who were destined for eternal life became believers. Thus the word of the Lord spread through the whole countryside.

But the Jews worked upon some of the devout women of the upper classes and the leading men of the city, and persuaded them to turn against Paul and Barnabas and expel them from their territory. So they shook the dust from their feet in defiance and went off to Iconium; but the disciples were filled with joy and the Holy Spirit.

R. The Word of the Lord.

Psalm 147:5–7

The leader prays a brief psalm.

The Lord is great and mighty in power;
his wisdom is beyond measure.
The Lord lifts up the humble,
but casts the wicked to the ground.
Sing to the Lord with thanksgiving,
make music on the harp for our God.

Our Father

The leader introduces the Lord's Prayer.

We commend all whom we love, or who have been entrusted to our prayers, to the unfailing love of God, and say together, as Christ himself has taught us:

R. *Our Father, who art in heaven,*
hallowed be thy name;
thy kingdom come;
thy will be done
on earth as it is in heaven.
Give us this day our daily bread,
and forgive us our trespasses,
as we forgive those who trespass
against us,
and lead us not into temptation,
but deliver us from evil.
Amen.

Second Reading

The leader reads this brief quotation.

Christ's Resurrection, if regarded so exclusively as *past,* finds its vision is limited to the empty tomb. But if the Resurrection is progressive, and based on Christ's victory over death, then it affects me *now….* The Resurrection is not just something that happened; it is something still happening.

FULTON J. SHEEN

Prayer to Give Good Example

The leader shares this prayer with those present.

Let us pray that through us
others may find the way of life in Christ.

Father,
we come, reborn in the Spirit,
to celebrate our sonship in the Lord Jesus Christ.
Touch our hearts,
help them grow towards the life you have promised.
Touch our lives,
make them signs of your love for all people.
We ask this through Jesus the Lord.
> *R. Amen.*

Let us remember in these prayers all who are sick and in need, our doctors, nurses, and caregivers, all our relatives and friends, living and dead, and the souls of all those recently deceased, as we seek the intercession of the Holy Mother of God, and say together:

> *R. Hail Mary, full of grace,*
> *the Lord is with thee.*
> *Blessed art thou among women*
> *and blessed is the fruit*
> *of thy womb Jesus.*
> *Holy Mary, Mother of God,*
> *pray for us sinners,*
> *now and at the hour of our death.*
> *Amen.*

Prayer to Take Up Christ's Cross

Those assembled make the sign of the cross, and the leader says this final prayer.

Lord Jesus,
may I seek always to defend your Church,
And to work tirelessly for the building up
of your kingdom here on earth.

Grant me the courage to take up your cross so that,
following in your way,
I may come to know the glory
of the Kingdom of Heaven,
where you live and reign with the Father
and the Holy Spirit, one God, for ever and ever.
    R. Amen.

The leader concludes by saying to those present:

May the Lord be with you always,
to be your strength and your peace.
    R. Thanks be to God.

Easter Week 4

This Sunday, sometimes known as Good Shepherd Sunday, is traditionally set aside by the Church for the people to pray for vocations to the religious life.

Greeting

The leader offers a greeting to all present.

May the grace of our Lord Jesus Christ,
and the love of God,
and the fellowship of the Holy Spirit,
be with us all as we pray here together.
> R. Amen.

Gathering Prayer

The leader begins by saying this opening prayer.

Grant, O God, that the hearts of us, your faithful, will abide in joy and that we may find that following what you command is the only true force among the changing things of this world.
> R. Amen.

First Reading

The leader reads a passage from sacred Scripture. This text recalls Christ as the Good Shepherd.

A reading according to the Gospel of John 10:14–18

I am the good shepherd;
I know my own
and my own know me,
just as the Father knows me
and I know the Father;
and I lay down my life for my sheep.
And there are other sheep I have
that are not of this fold,
and these I have to lead as well.
They too will listen to my voice,
and there will be only one flock,
and one shepherd.

 R. The Gospel of the Lord.

Psalm 98:1–2

The leader prays a brief psalm.

Sing to the Lord a new song,
for he has done wonders;
his right hand, his holy arm,
has won victory for him.
The Lord has shown his salvation,
revealing his justice to the nations.

Our Father

The leader introduces the Lord's Prayer.

We commend all whom we love, or who have been entrusted to our prayers, to the unfailing love of God, and say together, as Christ himself has taught us:

R. *Our Father, who art in heaven,*
hallowed be thy name;
thy kingdom come;
thy will be done
on earth as it is in heaven.
Give us this day our daily bread,
and forgive us our trespasses
as we forgive those who trespass
against us,
and lead us not into temptation,
but deliver us from evil.
Amen.

Second Reading

The leader reads this brief quotation.

Jesus says: "Respond more quickly to my voice, I who await you, I who have loved you for so long. Leave all. Let there no longer be anything else in the world for you but the love between you and me. Give, simplify your life, free yourself. Be all together poor so as to be altogether mine. Be more simple. Show yourself as you are….He should be able to read your heart without any effort, like an open book."

SISTER MARY OF THE HOLY TRINITY

Prayer for Healing

The leader shares this prayer with those present.

Lord,
you invite all who are burdened to come to you.
Allow your healing hand to heal me.
Touch my soul with your compassion for others.
Touch my heart with your infinite love for all.
Touch my mind with your wisdom,
that my mouth may always proclaim your praise.
Teach me to reach out to you in my need,
and help me to lead others to you by my example.
Most loving Heart of Jesus,
bring me health in body and spirit
that I may serve you with all my strength.
Touch gently this life, which you have created,
now and forever.
    R. Amen.

Let us remember in these prayers all who are sick and in need, our doctors, nurses, and caregivers, all our relatives and friends, living and dead, and the souls of all those recently deceased, as we seek the intercession of the Holy Mother of God, and say together:

> *R. Hail Mary, full of grace,*
> *the Lord is with thee.*
> *Blessed art thou among women*
> *and blessed is the fruit*
> *of thy womb Jesus.*

Holy Mary, Mother of God,
pray for us sinners,
now and at the hour of our death.
Amen.

Prayer for Vocations and Service

Making the sign of the cross, the leader says this prayer.

Lord Jesus, the Good Shepherd,
who offered your life that all might have life,
grant to us, the community of believers
throughout the world,
the abundance of your life,
the ability to witness it
and to communicate it to others.

Lord Jesus, grant the abundance of your life
to all those whom you are calling to your service,
especially young men and women.
Enlighten them in making their choices;
help them in their difficulties;
support them in faithfulness;
make them enthusiastic and courageous
in offering their lives in accord with your example.
    R. *Amen.*

The leader concludes by saying to those present:

May the Lord be with you always,
to be your strength and your peace.
    R. *Thanks be to God.*

Easter Week 5

Greeting

The leader offers a greeting to all present.

May the grace of our Lord Jesus Christ,
and the love of God,
and the fellowship of the Holy Spirit,
be with us all as we pray here together.
    R. Amen.

Gathering Prayer

The leader begins by saying this opening prayer.

May your Resurrection, O Lord, give us a renewed life in your grace, and may we be ever-mindful of our final goal of happiness with you in heaven.
    R. Amen.

First Reading

The leader reads a passage from sacred Scripture. The theme of this text is love.

A reading from the Letter of Paul to the Romans 8:35, 37–39

Nothing can come between us and the love of Christ, even if we are troubled or worried, or being persecuted, or lacking food or clothes, or being threatened or even attacked….These are the trials through which we triumph, by the power of him who loved us.

For I am certain of this: neither death nor life, no angel, no prince, nothing that exists, nothing still to come, not any power, or height or depth, nor any created thing, can ever come between us and the love of God made visible in Christ Jesus our Lord.

R. *The Word of the Lord.*

Psalm 84:5, 12

The leader prays a brief psalm.

Happy are those who live in your house,
continually singing your praise…!
For the Lord God is a sun and a shield;
he bestows favor and glory.
The Lord withholds no good thing
from those who walk in uprightness.

Our Father

The leader introduces the Lord's Prayer.

We commend all whom we love, or who have been entrusted to our prayers, to the unfailing love of God, and say together, as Christ himself has taught us:

R. Our Father, who art in heaven,
hallowed be thy name;
thy kingdom come;
thy will be done,
on earth as it is in heaven.
Give us this day our daily bread,
and forgive us our trespasses,
as we forgive those who trespass
against us,
and lead us not into temptation,
but deliver us from evil.
Amen.

Second Reading

The leader reads this brief quotation.

Be careful to give no credit to yourself for anything; if you do so, you are stealing from God, to whom alone every good thing is due. Strive to be lowly, to love your own insignificance, and to be ready to accept contempt and disgrace in defiance of human nature, which always longs for success and celebrity. This is the means beyond all other to become the servant of God, and to draw down the special blessing of heaven upon all your labor.

SAINT VINCENT DE PAUL

Prayer for the Spirit of Love

The leader shares this prayer with those present.

Almighty and ever-living God,
your Spirit made us your children and
gives us the confidence to call you Father.
Increase your Spirit within us,
and bring us to our promised inheritance.
Let us pray that through us,
others might find the way of life in Christ.
Father, we come reborn in the Spirit,
to celebrate our sonship in the Lord Jesus Christ.
Touch our hearts,
help them grow towards the life you have promised.
Touch our lives,
make them signs of your love for all people.
We ask this through your Son, Jesus Christ our Lord.
  R. *Amen.*

Let us remember in these prayers all who are sick
and in need, our doctors, nurses, and caregivers, all our
relatives and friends, living and dead, and the souls of
all those recently deceased, as we seek the intercession
of the Holy Mother of God, and say together:

  R. *Hail Mary, full of grace,*
     the Lord is with thee.
     Blessed art thou among women
     and blessed is the fruit
     of thy womb Jesus.

Holy Mary, Mother of God,
pray for us sinners,
now and at the hour of our death.
Amen.

Prayer for Help

Those assembled make the sign of the cross, and the leader says this prayer.

God, our Father,
make us one in Christ.
Help us to bring your salvation and joy
to all the world.
God, our Father,
be our help in human weakness,
show our sick brothers and sisters
the power of your loving care.
In your kindness, give them
all your graces and blessings.
We ask this through Christ our Lord.
    R. *Amen.*

The leader concludes by saying to those present:

May the Lord be with you always,
to be your strength and your peace.
    R. *Thanks be to God.*

Easter Week 6

Greeting

The leader offers a greeting to all present.

May the grace of our Lord Jesus Christ,
and the love of God,
and the fellowship of the Holy Spirit,
be with us all as we pray here together.
> *R. Amen.*

Gathering Prayer

The leader begins by saying this opening prayer.

Almighty God, whose love and kindness we rely on in our every suffering, grant that your protection will be with us unfailingly and may we be prepared and strengthened against all adversity.
> *R. Amen.*

First Reading

The leader reads a passage from sacred Scripture. The theme of this text is the gift of the Eucharist.

A reading from the Gospel according to John 6:30–35

The people said to Jesus: "What sign will you give to show us that we should believe in you? What work will you do? Our fathers had manna to eat in the desert; as scripture says: *He gave them bread from heaven to eat.*

Jesus answered: "I tell you most solemnly, it was not Moses who gave you bread from heaven. It is my father who gives you the bread from heaven, the true bread; for the bread of God is that which comes down from heaven and gives life to the world."

"Sir," they said, "give us that bread always."

Jesus answered: "I am the bread of life. He who comes to me will never be hungry; he who believes in me will never thirst."

R. The Gospel of the Lord.

Psalm 109:26, 30–31

The leader prays a brief psalm.

Help me, O Lord my God,
and save me for the sake of your love....
To the Lord, I will give my thanks;
I will praise him in the great assembly.
He stands at the right hand of the needy.

Our Father

The leader introduces the Lord's Prayer.

We commend all whom we love, or who have been entrusted to our prayers, to the unfailing love of God, and say together, as Christ himself has taught us:

R. *Our Father, who art in heaven,*
hallowed be thy name;
thy kingdom come;
thy will be done
on earth as it is in heaven.
Give us this day our daily bread,
and forgive us our trespasses
as we forgive those who trespass
against us,
and lead us not into temptation,
but deliver us from evil.
Amen.

Second Reading

The leader reads this brief quotation.

The heart of the true servant of God must be like an altar, on which is offered the gold of the most ardent charity, the incense of continual prayer, and the myrrh of incessant mortification. If our salvation was left in our own hands, we should have very great reason to fear; but, as it is in the hands of God, who is our Father, we may rest with tranquility in him. When our sins terrify us, and we fear being damned, let us think on the merits of the crucified, and our spirit will be refreshed.

SAINT PAUL OF THE CROSS

Prayer to Avert Discouragement

The leader shares this prayer with those present.

Let us pray
for all who are discouraged
by the hardness of human beings,
that they may not hate the light of life
and become embittered,
and think that evil is stronger than good,
but that they may keep an open heart
in hope and expectation.
Lord, graciously hear us.
   R. Amen.

Let us remember in these prayers all who are sick and in need, our doctors, nurses, and caregivers, all our relatives and friends, living and dead, and the souls of all those recently deceased, as we seek the intercession of the Holy Mother of God, and say together:

R. Hail Mary, full of grace,
   the Lord is with thee.
   Blessed art thou among women
   and blessed is the fruit
   of thy womb Jesus.
   Holy Mary, Mother of God,
   pray for us sinners,
   now and at the hour of our death.
   Amen.

Prayer for Those Unable to Receive Communion

Those assembled make the sign of the cross, and the leader says this final prayer.

My brothers and sisters:
Before our Lord Jesus Christ passed from this world
to return to his Father,
he gave us the sacrament of his Body and Blood.
This is the promise of our resurrection,
the food and drink for our journey
as we pass from this life to join him.
United in the love of Christ,
let us ask God to give strength to us all
and to our brothers and sisters in Christ
who, for whatever reason,
are unable to receive this sacrament.
    R. Amen.

The leader concludes by saying to those present:

May the Lord be with you always,
to be your strength and your peace.
    R. Thanks be to God.

Easter Week 7

Greeting

The leader offers a greeting to all present.

May the grace of our Lord Jesus Christ,
and the love of God,
and the fellowship of the Holy Spirit,
be with us all as we pray here together.
    R. *Amen.*

Gathering Prayer

The leader begins by saying this opening prayer.

    Father, may we turn our efforts toward knowing you deeply through prayer, and may all who are sick and suffering be given the hope of good things to come.
    R. *Amen.*

First Reading

The leader reads a passage from sacred Scripture. The theme of this text is trust in the Lord.

A reading from the Gospel according to
John 14:6–14

Jesus said to Thomas: "I am the Way, the Truth and the Life. No one can come to the Father except through me.

"If you know me, you know my Father too. From this moment you know him and have seen him."

Philip said, "Lord, let us see the Father and then we shall be satisfied." "Have I been with you all this time, Philip," said Jesus to him, "and you still do not know me?"

"To have seen me is to have seen the Father, so how can you say, 'Let us see the Father?' Do you not believe that I am in the Father and the Father is in me? The words I say to you I do not speak as from myself: it is the Father, living in me, who is doing this work. You must believe me when I say that I am in the Father and the Father is in me; believe it on the evidence of this work, if for no other reason. I tell you most solemnly, whoever believes in me will perform the same works as I do myself, he will perform ever greater works, because I am going to the Father. Whatever you ask for in my name I will do, so that the Father may be glorified in the Son. If you ask for anything in my name, I will do it."

R. The Gospel of the Lord.

Psalm 30:5, 10, 12

The leader prays a brief psalm.

Sing to the Lord, O you his saints,
give thanks and praise to his holy name….
"What good would there be in my destruction,
in my going down to the pit?
Would my dust give you praise…?"
But now, you have turned my mourning
into rejoicing;
you have taken off my sackcloth and
wrapped me in the garments of gladness.

Our Father

The leader introduces the Lord's Prayer.

We commend all whom we love, or who have been
entrusted to our prayers, to the unfailing love of God,
and say together, as Christ himself has taught us:

> R. *Our Father, who art in heaven,*
> *hallowed be thy name;*
> *thy kingdom come;*
> *thy will be done on earth as it is in heaven.*
> *Give us this day our daily bread,*
> *and forgive us our trespasses,*
> *as we forgive those who trespass against us,*
> *and lead us not into temptation,*
> *but deliver us from evil.*
> *Amen.*

Second Reading

The leader reads this brief quotation.

If evil people revile us, let us console ourselves with the thought that God will bless and praise us. To be praised by God, by Mary, by the angels, by the saints, or even by ordinary good people, should be enough for us. The greater the opposition we meet in doing good, the more we shall please God. Let us never be embarrassed in appearing as Christians.

SAINT ALPHONSUS LIGUORI

Erasmus's Prayer for Guidance

The leader shares this prayer with those present.

O Lord Jesus Christ,
who are the Way, the Truth, and the Life,
we pray thee suffer us
not to stray from you who are the Way,
nor to distrust you who are the Truth,
nor to rest in any other thing than you,
who are the Life.
Teach us by your Holy Spirit what to believe,
what to do, and wherein to take our rest.
   R. Amen.

Let us remember in these prayers all who are sick and in need, our doctors, nurses, and caregivers, all our relatives and friends, living and dead, and the souls of all those recently deceased, as we seek the intercession of the Holy Mother of God, and say together:

R. *Hail Mary, full of grace,*
the Lord is with thee.
Blessed art thou among women
and blessed is the fruit
of thy womb Jesus.
Holy Mary, Mother of God,
pray for us sinners,
now and at the hour of our death.
Amen.

Prayer for Support in Sickness

Those assembled make the sign of the cross, and the leader says this final prayer.

Almighty and ever-living Lord,
you restored us to life
by raising Christ from death.
Strengthen us by this Easter event;
may we feel its saving power in our daily life.
We ask this through Christ our Lord.
  R. Amen.

The leader concludes by saying to those present:

May the Lord be with you always,
to be your strength and your peace.
  R. Thanks be to God.

Ascension of Our Lord

This holy day of obligation falls forty days after Easter and commemorates the Ascension of Christ into heaven. In many dioceses of the United States, this celebration is transferred to the following Sunday.

Greeting

The leader offers a greeting to all present.

May the grace of our Lord Jesus Christ,
and the love of God,
and the fellowship of the Holy Spirit,
be with us all as we pray here together.
> R. Amen.

Gathering Prayer

The leader begins by saying this opening prayer.

Praise to you, O Lord, who has been lifted up victoriously to the Father; intercede for us and give us the grace to follow you and bring our journey to its rightful conclusion with you in heaven.
> R. Amen.

First Reading

The leader reads a passage from sacred Scripture. This text recounts Christ's Ascension into heaven.

A reading from the Gospel according to
Luke 24:46–53

Jesus said to his two disciples:

"You see how it is written that the Christ would suffer and on the third day rise from the dead, and that, in his name, repentance for the forgiveness of sins would be preached to all the nations, beginning from Jerusalem. You are witnesses to this. "And now I am sending down to you what the father has promised. Stay in the city then, until you are clothed with the power from on high." Then he took them out as far as the outskirts of Bethany, and lifting up his hands he blessed them. Now as he blessed them, he withdrew from them and was carried up to heaven.

They worshiped him and then went back to Jerusalem full of joy; and they were continually in the Temple praising God.

R. The Gospel of the Lord.

Psalm 68:33–35

The leader prays a brief psalm.

Sing to God, O kingdoms of the world;
sing praises to the Lord,
to him who rides the ancient heavens and
speaks in the voice of thunder.
Proclaim the might of God;
he is great in Israel, powerful in heavens.

Our Father

The leader introduces the Lord's Prayer.

We commend all whom we love, or who have been entrusted to our prayers, to the unfailing love of God, and say together, as Christ himself has taught us:

R. *Our Father, who art in heaven,*
   hallowed be thy name;
   thy kingdom come;
   thy will be done
   on earth as it is in heaven.
   Give us this day our daily bread,
   and forgive us our trespasses,
   as we forgive those who trespass
   against us,
   and lead us not into temptation,
   but deliver us from evil.
   Amen.

Second Reading

The leader reads this brief quotation.

Jesus has no riches, no possessions, not even a home. He has not whereon to rest his head. They who expect from him temporal goods will receive nothing. His cross, his nails, his crown of thorns—behold his earthly estate! Ah, if Our Lord gave earthly riches, how many good Christians there would be! Who would not be his disciple…?

And yet, Our Lord wishes to make a will. And of what? Of himself! He is God, he is Master of his sacred humanity. He gives that to us, and with it all that he is. He really gives it to us. It is not a loan; it is a gift.

He becomes bread: his Body, his Blood, his Soul, and his Divinity taking the place of the substance of the bread offered. Though we see him not, we possess him.

SAINT PETER JULIAN EYMARD

Prayer to the Ascended Christ

The leader shares this prayer with those present.

King of Glory, Lord Almighty,
today you have ascended victoriously
above the heavens.
Do not leave us as orphans without a guide,
but send the one whom you promised,
the gift of the Father, the Spirit of Truth. Alleluia!
    R. *Amen.*

Let us remember in these prayers all who are sick and in need, our doctors, nurses, and caregivers, all our relatives and friends, living and dead, and the souls of all those recently deceased, as we seek the intercession of the Holy Mother of God, and say together:

R. *Hail Mary, full of grace,
    the Lord is with thee.
    Blessed art thou among women
    and blessed is the fruit
    of thy womb Jesus.*

Holy Mary, Mother of God,
pray for us sinners,
now and at the hour of our death.
Amen.

Prayer for Renewal

Those assembled make the sign of the cross, and the leader says this final prayer.

Come, Holy Spirit, fill the hearts of your faithful
and enkindle in them the fire of your love.
Send forth your Spirit and they shall be created,
and you shall renew the face of the earth.

Let us pray,
O God, who has taught the hearts of the faithful
by the light of the Holy Spirit,
grant that by the gift of the same Spirit
we may be always truly wise
and ever rejoice in his consolation.
    R. *Amen.*

The leader concludes by saying to those present:

May the Lord be with you always,
to be your strength and your peace.
    R. *Thanks be to God.*

Pentecost

Pentecost is observed fifty days after Easter and commemorates the descent of the Holy Spirit upon the apostles. It is regarded as the birthday of the Catholic Church. In some communities, this Sunday is also observed as a "Day of suffering for the missions."

Greeting

The leader offers a greeting to all present.

May the grace of our Lord Jesus Christ,
and the love of God,
and the fellowship of the Holy Spirit,
be with us all as we pray here together.
    R. Amen.

Gathering Prayer

The leader begins by saying this opening prayer.

Lord of heaven and earth, you inspire and bring us together through the gift of the Spirit, give our mortal bodies the life that is never ending.
    R. Amen.

First Reading and Response

The leader reads a passage from sacred Scripture. This text recounts the descent of the Holy Spirit on the Apostles.

A reading from the Acts of the Apostles 2:1–11

When Pentecost day came round, the apostles had all met in one room, when suddenly they heard what sounded like a powerful wind from heaven, the noise of which filled the entire house in which they were sitting; and something appeared to them that seemed like tongues of fire; these separated and came to rest on the head of each of them.

They were all filled with the Holy Spirit, and began to speak foreign languages as the Spirit gave them the gift of speech.

Now there were devout men living in Jerusalem from every nation under heaven, and at this sound they all assembled, each one bewildered to hear these men speaking his own language. They were amazed and astonished.

"Surely" they said, "all these men speaking are Galileans? How does it happen that each of us hears them in his own native language? Parthians, Medes and Elamites; people from Mesopotamia, Judaea and Cappadocia, Pontus and Asia, Phrygia and Pamphylia, Egypt and parts of Libya round Cyrene; as well as visitors from Rome—Jews and proselytes alike—Cretans and Arabs; we hear them preaching in our own language about the marvels of God."

R. The Word of the Lord.

Psalm 105:27–30

The leader prays a brief psalm.

They all look to you
for their food in due time.
You give it to them,
and they gather it up;
you open your hand,
they are filled with good things.
When you hide your face they vanish,
you take away their breath,
they expire and return to dust.
When you send forth your spirit,
they are created,
and the face of the earth is renewed.

Our Father

The leader introduces the Lord's Prayer.

We commend all whom we love, or who have been
entrusted to our prayers, to the unfailing love of God,
and say together, as Christ himself has taught us:

> *R. Our Father, who art in heaven,*
> *hallowed be thy name;*
> *thy kingdom come;*
> *thy will be done on earth as it is in heaven.*
> *Give us this day our daily bread,*
> *and forgive us our trespasses,*
> *as we forgive those who trespass against us,*
> *and lead us not into temptation,*
> *but deliver us from evil.*
> *Amen.*

Second Reading

The leader reads this brief quotation.

Finally, the happy moment [the sacrament of confirmation] arrived. I did not feel a brisk wind when the Holy Spirit descended, but instead, I felt that light breeze on which the Prophet Elijah heard the whisper on Mount Horeb….On that day, I received the strength to suffer.

SAINT THÉRÈSE OF LISIEUX

Prayer to the Holy Spirit

The leader shares this prayer with those present.

Let us pray in the Spirit
that we may grow in the love of God.
Almighty and ever-living God,
your spirit made us, your children,
confident to call you Father.
Increase your Spirit within us
and bring us to our promised inheritance.
We ask this through Christ our Lord.
    R. Amen.

Let us remember in these prayers all who are sick and in need, and also the doctors, the nurses, the caregivers, all our relatives and friends, living and dead, and the souls of all those recently deceased, as we seek the intercession of the Holy Mother of God, and say together:

R. Hail Mary, full of grace,
the Lord is with thee.
Blessed art thou among women
and blessed is the fruit
of thy womb Jesus.
Holy Mary, Mother of God,
pray for us sinners,
now and at the hour of our death.
Amen.

The Holy Spirit—A Petition

Making the sign of the cross, the leader says this prayer.

O God, our Father,
on the first Pentecost
you opened the hearts of those
who believed in you
by the light of the Holy Spirit.
In the same Holy Spirit, give us a desire
for what is right and just,
and a continuing sense of his presence
and power in our lives.
We ask this through Christ our Lord.
R. *Amen.*

The leader concludes by saying to those present:

May the Lord be with you always,
to be your strength and your peace.
R. *Thanks be to God.*

Holy Trinity

This solemnity is a movable observance held on the Sunday after Pentecost. It commemorates the mystery of three Divine Persons in one God.

Greeting

The leader offers a greeting to all present.

May the grace of our Lord Jesus Christ,
and the love of God,
and the fellowship of the Holy Spirit,
be with us all as we pray here together.
    R. *Amen.*

Gathering Prayer

The leader begins by saying this opening prayer.

O One and Holy God, you who are the life of the living and the dead, let us dwell with the Father, Son, and Holy Spirit in fellowship and love.
    R. *Amen.*

First Reading

The leader reads a passage from sacred Scripture. The theme of this text is discipleship.

A reading from the Gospel according to
Matthew 28:16–20

Meanwhile, the eleven disciples set out for Galilee, to the mountain where Jesus had arranged to meet them. When they saw him they fell down before him, though some hesitated.

Jesus came up and spoke to them. He said, "All authority in heaven and on earth has been given to me. Go, therefore, make disciples of all the nations; baptize them in the name of the Father and of the Son and of the Holy Spirit, and teach them to observe all the commands I gave you. And know that I am with you always, yes, to the end of time."

R. The Gospel of the Lord.

Psalm 68:5, 8–9

The leader prays a brief psalm.

Sing to God,
sing praises to his name;
open the way to him
who rides upon the clouds;
the Lord is his name.
Rejoice in his presence....
O God, when you went forth to lead
your people through the desert,
the earth trembled,
the heavens poured down rain.

Our Father

The leader introduces the Lord's Prayer.

We commend all whom we love, or who have been entrusted to our prayers, to the unfailing love of God, and say together, as Christ himself has taught us:

R. Our Father, who art in heaven,
hallowed be thy name;
thy kingdom come;
thy will be done
on earth as it is in heaven.
Give us this day our daily bread,
and forgive us our trespasses,
as we forgive those who trespass
against us,
and lead us not into temptation,
but deliver us from evil.
Amen.

Second Reading

The leader reads this brief quotation.

Do not be afraid; holiness does not happen in one day or one year. It requires simplicity, purity, abandonment. Such is the way, the most perfect of all, that is given to you and me by the Father, Son, and the Holy Spirit.

JOHANNES TAULER

Prayer for Healing

The leader shares this prayer with those present.

Almighty and eternal God,
who pours into broken bodies
the healing graces of your own blessing
and in a thousand ways shows your care
for what your hands have made,
be good to us and draw near
as we call upon your name.
Deliver your servants from their sickness.
Give them health anew.
Stretch out your hand
and set them on their feet again.
Put strength into them and keep them safe
under your powerful protection.
We ask this through Christ our Lord.
  R. Amen.

Let us remember in these prayers all who are sick
and in need, our doctors, nurses, and caregivers, all our
relatives and friends, living and dead, and the souls of
all those recently deceased, as we seek the intercession
of the Holy Mother of God, and say together:

R. Hail Mary, full of grace,
the Lord is with thee.
Blessed art thou among women
and blessed is the fruit
of thy womb Jesus.

Holy Mary, Mother of God,
pray for us sinners,
now and at the hour of our death.
Amen.

John McQuiggan's Prayer for Strength in Suffering

Those assembled make the sign of the cross, and the leader says this prayer.

Dear God,
We do not understand
why some of us must suffer so much.
But we know that
your Son, Jesus, suffered for our sake.
In our sufferings, Lord,
give us the strength to share what we can,
and to sustain what we must.
We ask this through Christ our Lord.
     R. *Amen.*

The leader concludes by saying to those present:

May the Lord be with you always,
to be your strength and your peace.
     R. *Thanks be to God.*

The Body and Blood of Christ
(Corpus Christi)

In the United States, this movable celebration is held on the Sunday following Trinity Sunday and commemorates the institution of the Holy Eucharist.

Greeting

The leader offers a greeting to all present.

May the grace of our Lord Jesus Christ,
and the love of God,
and the fellowship of the Holy Spirit
be with us all as we pray here together.
    R. Amen.

Gathering Prayer

The leader begins by saying this opening prayer.

O God, we thank you for your gift of the sacrament of the Eucharist. May your body and blood be a constant reminder of our oneness in Christ.
    R. Amen.

First Reading

The leader reads a passage from sacred Scripture. This text recounts the institution of the Holy Eucharist.

A reading from the First Letter of Paul to the Corinthians 11:23–26.

This is what I received from the Lord and passed on to you: that on the same night he was betrayed, the Lord Jesus took some bread, and thanked God for it and broke it, and he said, "This is my Body, which is for you; do this as a memorial of me."

In the same way he took the cup after supper, and said, "This cup is the new covenant in my Blood. Whenever you drink it, do this as a memorial of me."

Until the Lord comes, therefore, every time you eat this bread and drink this cup you are proclaiming his death.

R. The Word of the Lord.

Psalm 105:40–42, 43

The leader prays a brief psalm.

They asked for food;
he gave them quails and
fed them with bread from heaven.
He opened the rock, and water gushed out,
flowing like a river through the desert....
So he led forth his people with joy,
his chosen ones with singing.

Our Father

The leader introduces the Lord's Prayer.

We commend all whom we love, or who have been entrusted to our prayers, to the unfailing love of God, and say together, as Christ himself has taught us:

R. *Our Father, who art in heaven,*
hallowed be thy name;
thy kingdom come;
thy will be done on earth as it is in heaven.
Give us this day our daily bread,
and forgive us our trespasses,
as we forgive those who trespass
against us,
and lead us not into temptation,
but deliver us from evil.
Amen.

Second Reading

The leader reads this brief quotation.

God wants to awake all the dead to life, not merely on the last day, but even now. Every person who is stuck in his or her ego, who does whatever it takes to get his or her way, who doesn't listen to God's Spirit of love, is actually more dead than alive. But God wants to awake us all to life, many times a day. It is all a matter of letting oneself be awoken.

WILFRID STINISSEN, O. CARM.

Prayer for Charity

The leader shares this prayer with those present.

> May our pilgrimage of faith,
> inspired by hope,
> manifest charity in abundance,
> so that God's will
> may be known in our lives.
> May we reflect in every thought, word, and action
> the life of the Kingdom
> prepared for those who love you.
> We make this prayer through Christ our Lord.
> *R. Amen.*

Let us remember in these prayers all who are sick and in need, our doctors, nurses, and caregivers, all our relatives and friends, living and dead, and the souls of all those recently deceased, as we seek the intercession of the Holy Mother of God, and say together:

> *R. Hail Mary, full of grace,*
> *the Lord is with thee.*
> *Blessed art thou among women*
> *and blessed is the fruit*
> *of thy womb Jesus.*
> *Holy Mary, Mother of God,*
> *pray for us sinners,*
> *now and at the hour of our death.*
> *Amen.*

Prayer for Renewal

Those assembled make the sign of the cross, and the leader says this final prayer.

Lord, we are renewed
by the breaking of one bread.
Keep us in your love
and help us to live
the new life Christ won for us.
Grant this in the name of Jesus the Lord.
    R. Amen.

The leader concludes by saying to those present:

May the Lord be with you always,
to be your strength and your peace.
    R. Thanks be to God.

Birth of John the Baptist

This solemnity is held on June 24 and commemorates the birthday of Christ's cousin and his precursor.

Greeting

The leader offers a greeting to all present.

May the grace of our Lord Jesus Christ,
and the love of God,
and the fellowship of the Holy Spirit,
be with us all as we pray here together.
    R. Amen.

Gathering Prayer

The leader begins by saying this opening prayer.

Father of fire and light, may we all be witnesses to the coming of Christ just as John the Baptist heralded the arrival of the Word. May our hearts never fail in this journey of faith, and may we follow you as faithfully and hopefully as did John.
    R. Amen.

First Reading

The leader reads a passage from sacred Scripture. The theme of this text is John the Baptist's proclamation of Christ's arrival.

Paul said: "God made David the king of our ancestors, of whom he approved in these words, 'I have elected David, son of Jesse, a man after my own heart, who will carry out my whole purpose.'

"To keep his promise, God has raised up for Israel one of David's descendants, Jesus, as Savior, whose coming was heralded by John when he proclaimed a baptism of repentance for the whole people of Israel.

"Before John ended his career he said, 'I am not the one you imagine me to be; that one is coming after me and I am not fit to undo his sandal.' My brothers, sons of Abraham's race, and all you who fear God, this message of salvation is meant for you."

R. *The Word of the Lord.*

Psalm 97:1, 3–4

The leader prays a brief psalm.

The Lord reigns,
let the earth rejoice;
let the distant islands be glad....
Fire goes before him,
burning his foes on every side.
His lightning lights up the world;
the earth watches and trembles.

Our Father

The leader introduces the Lord's Prayer.

We commend all whom we love, or who have been entrusted to our prayers, to the unfailing love of God, and say together, as Christ himself has taught us:

R. *Our Father, who art in heaven,*
hallowed be thy name;
thy kingdom come;
thy will be done on earth as it is in heaven.
Give us this day our daily bread,
and forgive us our trespasses,
as we forgive those who trespass against us,
and lead us not into temptation,
but deliver us from evil.
Amen.

Second Reading

The leader reads this brief quotation.

We have only the present, and it is at that moment that God is waiting to give himself to us. It is today that we must listen to his voice. It is now that we must make ourselves available to him. It is easy to fix our gaze on the past, and it is easy to make plans for the future. But we don't live in our yesterdays or in our tomorrows; we only live in the present. The present is not ours to waste, for it belongs to God.

BROTHER VICTOR-ANTOINE D'AVILA-LATOURRETTE

Prayer to Fight Fear

The leader shares this prayer with those present.

Though the powers of darkness threaten to fill us with fear, we must remember that they are nothing compared with the power of Jesus, the Lord of the universe. Even more, our sins may so frighten us that we do not look at them and are afraid even to repent of them.

Nevertheless, let us fix our eyes on Jesus. The love that comes from him is more powerful than our sin. His Blood has freed us—personally and collectively—of the web of sin and bondage we have woven ourselves. He has died for us.

Jesus Christ is for us—individually and as a body of believers—right now, the manifestation of the mercy of God. Let us go to him and receive grace and mercy in time of need. May our hearts be filled with faith: How wonderful are your works, O Lord: the whole world is filled with your gracious mercy!

R. Amen.

Let us remember in these prayers all who are sick and in need, our doctors, nurses, and caregivers, all our relatives and friends, living and dead, and the souls of all those recently deceased, as we seek the intercession of the Holy Mother of God, and say together:

*R. Hail Mary, full of grace,
the Lord is with thee.
Blessed art thou among women
and blessed is the fruit of thy womb Jesus.*

Holy Mary, Mother of God,
pray for us sinners,
now and at the hour of our death.
Amen.

Prayer for Belief

Those assembled make the sign of the cross, and the leader says this final prayer.

For our part, because of our Christian faith,
we look to Jesus as our primary guide to God.
He tells us his Father's secrets.
He gives us a taste of living,
living now and eternally.
We have to discover the God
who speaks a name and shows us a face.
Let us believe in the God of Jesus Christ,
our brother, our friend, our Savior.
    R. *Amen.*

The leader concludes by saying to those present:

May the Lord be with you always,
to be your strength and your peace.
    R. *Thanks be to God.*

Saints Peter and Paul

This solemnity held on June 29 is a joint commemoration of the martyrdom of these two apostles.

Greeting

The leader offers a greeting to all present.

May the grace of our Lord Jesus Christ,
and the love of God,
and the fellowship of the Holy Spirit,
be with us all as we pray here together.
> *R. Amen.*

Gathering Prayer

The leader begins by saying this opening prayer.

O God, may the words of your apostles Peter and Paul, to whom this day is consecrated, settle soundly in our hearts. May we follow in their footsteps and may we, by our conduct, spread the Good News to all who enter our lives.
> *R. Amen.*

First Reading

The leader reads a passage from sacred Scripture. This text is about patience in suffering.

A reading from the Letter of Paul to the Romans 5:1–5

Through our Lord Jesus Christ, by faith we are judged righteous and at peace with God, since it is by faith and through Jesus that we have entered this state of grace in which we can boast about looking forward to God's glory. But that is not all we can boast about; we can boast about our sufferings. These sufferings bring patience, as we know, and patience brings perseverance, and perseverance brings hope, and this hope is not deceptive, because the love of God has been poured into our hearts by the Holy Spirit which has been given to us.

R. *The Word of the Lord.*

Psalm 19:2–3, 15

The leader prays a brief psalm.

The heavens declare the glory of God;
the firmament proclaims the work of his hands.
Day talks it over with day;
night hands on the knowledge to night....
May the words of my mouth
and the meditations of my heart
find favor in your sight, O Lord.

Our Father

The leader introduces the Lord's Prayer.

We commend all whom we love, or who have been entrusted to our prayers, to the unfailing love of God, and say together, as Christ himself has taught us:

R. *Our Father, who art in heaven,*
hallowed be thy name;
thy kingdom come;
thy will be done
on earth as it is in heaven.
Give us this day our daily bread,
and forgive us our trespasses,
as we forgive those who trespass
against us,
and lead us not into temptation,
but deliver us from evil.
Amen.

Second Reading

The leader reads this brief quotation.

Christ came not only to proclaim a message but to use a healing power. He wishes to heal because we have wounds which paralyze genuine love: wounds that make us deaf to his word, blind to what he wants us to see. His healing brings happiness and freedom so that we can carry our burdens and serve more faithfully.

BASIL HUME

Prayer to Alleviate Pain

The leader shares this prayer with those present.

Support and strengthen us, Lord!
Help us to keep going,
have mercy on all sinners.

We offer all our pain
against the terrible pain of the world.
Lord, we offer what we suffer
for those who suffer without hope,
and without faith.

Let us pray that everything we do
will be guided by God's law of love.
God, our Father,
you have promised to remain forever
with those who do what is just and right.
Help us to live in your presence.
We ask this through your Son, Jesus Christ.
    R. Amen.

    Let us remember in these prayers all who are sick and in need, our doctors, nurses, and caregivers, all our relatives and friends, living and dead, and the souls of all those recently deceased, as we seek the intercession of the Holy Mother of God, and say together:

R. *Hail Mary, full of grace,*
  the Lord is with thee.
  Blessed art thou among women
  and blessed is the fruit
  of thy womb Jesus.
  Holy Mary, Mother of God,
  pray for us sinners,
  now and at the hour of our death.
  Amen.

Prayer in the Face of Pain

Those assembled make the sign of the cross, and the leader says this final prayer.

Lord,
you have known the pain of suffering,
be with us in our pain,
and comfort us in our loneliness.
Forgive our impatience,
and bless our efforts to be generous to all.
  R. *Amen.*

The leader concludes by saying to those present:

May the Lord be with you always,
to be your strength and your peace.
  R. *Thanks be to God.*

Transfiguration of the Lord

Held on August 6, this feast commemorates the revelation of Christ's divinity to Peter, James, and John on Mount Tabor.

Greeting

The leader offers a greeting to all present.

May the grace of our Lord Jesus Christ,
and the love of God,
and the fellowship of the Holy Spirit,
be with us all as we pray here together.
    R. Amen.

Gathering Prayer

The leader begins by saying this opening prayer.

Eternal God, give us the grace to refigure our sufferings into joy just as Christ was transfigured on Mount Tabor. Reveal yourself and open our eyes to your glory.
    R. Amen.

First Reading

The leader reads a passage from sacred Scripture. This text recounts the events of Christ's Transfiguration.

Jesus took with him Peter and James and his brother John and led them up a high mountain where they could be alone.

There in their presence he was transfigured: his face shone like the sun and his clothes became as white as the light. Suddenly Moses and Elijah appeared to them; they were talking with him.

Then Peter spoke to Jesus. "Lord," he said "it is wonderful for us to be here; if you wish, I will make three tents here, one for you, one for Moses and one for Elijah." He was still speaking when suddenly a bright cloud covered them with a shadow, and from the cloud there came a voice, which said, "This is my Son, the Beloved; he enjoys my favor. Listen to him." When they heard this, the disciples fell on their faces, overcome with fear.

But Jesus came up and touched them. "Stand up," he said. "Do not be afraid." And when they raised their eyes they saw no one but only Jesus.

As they came down from the mountain Jesus gave them this order, "Tell no one about the vision until the Son of Man has risen from the dead."

R. *The Gospel of the Lord.*

Psalm 76:5, 9–10

The leader prays a brief psalm.

You are glorious and majestic,
enthroned on everlasting mountains….
You thundered judgment from the heavens;
while the earth trembled and lay still,
as you, O God, arose to judge,
to save all the humble of the earth.

Our Father

The leader introduces the Lord's Prayer.

We commend all whom we love, or who have been
entrusted to our prayers, to the unfailing love of God,
and say together, as Christ himself has taught us:

> *R. Our Father, who art in heaven,*
> *hallowed be thy name;*
> *thy kingdom come;*
> *thy will be done*
> *on earth as it is in heaven.*
> *Give us this day our daily bread,*
> *and forgive us our trespasses,*
> *as we forgive those who trespass*
> *against us,*
> *and lead us not into temptation,*
> *but deliver us from evil.*
> *Amen.*

Second Reading

The leader reads this brief quotation.

The name of Jesus is a concrete and powerful means of transfiguring human beings into their hidden, innermost, utmost reality. We should approach all men and women—in the street, the shop, the office, the factory and especially those who seem irritating and antipathetic—with the name of Jesus in our heart and on our lips. Name them with the name of Jesus in a spirit of adoration, dedication, and service. If we go through the world with this new vision, seeing Jesus in every person, everybody will be transformed and transfigured before our eyes.

WILFRID STINISSEN, O. CARM.

Prayer for Help in Sickness

The leader shares this prayer with those present.

Father, you decided that your Son
should bear our infirmities
so as to show us the power
of human weakness and endurance.
In your goodness,
hear the prayers that we make
for our brothers and sisters who are sick.

Help them to believe
that they have been numbered
among those whom your Son called blessed,
to be united with him in his suffering
for the salvation of the world.
Through Christ our Lord.

    R. Amen.

Let us remember in these prayers all who are sick and in need, our doctors, nurses, and caregivers, all our relatives and friends, living and dead, and the souls of all those recently deceased, as we seek the intercession of the Holy Mother of God, and say together:

    R. Hail Mary, full of grace,
       the Lord is with thee.
       Blessed art thou among women
       and blessed is the fruit of thy womb Jesus.
       Holy Mary, Mother of God,
       pray for us sinners,
       now and at the hour of our death.
       Amen.

Prayer for the Disabled

Those assembled make the sign of the cross, and the leader says this final prayer.

O loving Father,
we pray for all who face disabilities
in the race of life,
and all who are permanently injured.

We pray for those worn out with sickness
or wasted with misery,
for the dying, and for unhappy children.
May they learn the mystery of the road of suffering
which Christ has trodden
and the saints have followed,
and bring you this gift that angels cannot bring,
a heart that trusts you even in the dark.
This we ask in the name of him
who took our infirmities upon himself,
even the same Jesus our Savior.
　　R. Amen.

The leader concludes by saying to those present:

May the Lord be with you always,
to be your strength and your peace.
　　R. Thanks be to God.

Assumption of the Blessed Virgin Mary

This holy day of obligation, held on August 15, commemorates the assumption of Mary's soul and body into heaven.

Greeting

The leader offers a greeting to all present.

May the grace of our Lord Jesus Christ,
and the love of God,
and the fellowship of the Holy Spirit,
be with us all as we pray here together.
   R. *Amen.*

Gathering Prayer

The leader begins by saying this opening prayer.

Heavenly Father, through the intercession of the Virgin Mary, may our prayers rise to you as did the person of Mary, our Queen and Mother, whose feast we celebrate today. May all who are sick and infirm see the heavens open up to receive them just as they received the Mother of your Son home to you.
   R. *Amen.*

First Reading and Response

The leader reads a passage from sacred Scripture. This is the text of Mary's Magnificat.

A reading according to the Gospel of Luke 1:46–53

And Mary said:
"My soul proclaims the greatness of the Lord
and my spirit exults in God my Savior;
because he has looked upon his lowly handmaid.
Yes, from this day forward
all generations will call me blessed,
for the almighty has done great things for me.
Holy is his name,
and his mercy reaches from age to age
for those who fear him.
He has shown the power of his arm,
He has routed the proud of heart.
He has pulled down princes from their thrones
and exalted the lowly.
The hungry he has filled with good things,
the rich sent empty away."

 R. The Gospel of the Lord.

Psalm 24:3–5

The leader prays a brief psalm.

Who will ascend the mountain of the Lord?
Who will stand in his holy place?
Those with clean hands and pure heart,
who desire not what is vain….
They will receive blessings from the Lord,
a reward from God, their savior.

Our Father

The leader introduces the Lord's Prayer.

We commend all whom we love, or who have been entrusted to our prayers, to the unfailing love of God, and say together, as Christ himself has taught us:

R. Our Father, who art in heaven,
hallowed be thy name;
thy kingdom come;
thy will be done on earth as it is in heaven.
Give us this day our daily bread,
and forgive us our trespasses,
as we forgive those who trespass against us,
and lead us not into temptation,
but deliver us from evil.
Amen.

Second Reading

The leader reads this brief quotation.

God willed that the Blessed Virgin Mary play a central part in the Mystery of the Incarnation and of our Redemption. He willed that the salvation of the world should depend on her consent. Mary is the "royal way" by which the King of Glory descended into the world in order to restore fallen humankind to its destined place in heaven....We need her to go forth to meet our Savior on the same Road by which he came to us.

THOMAS MERTON

Prayer to Our Lady

The leader shares this prayer with those present.

O Glorious and ever Virgin Mary,
Mother of God,
look down with love and mercy on us.
We have come to honor you,
to show our love for you,
and, especially, to rejoice with you
in your assumption into heaven.

We give thanks to the Most Holy Trinity
for choosing you from among all women
to be Mother of God.
Our souls, like yours, glorify the Lord,
for he is mighty,
and has done great things for you;
Holy is his name.
Now, O Mary, Queen of the Church,
and our loving Mother,
hear our prayers and offer them
with your own on our behalf to God.

If it is his holy will, obtain for us
the graces for which we ask.
Grant also that our prayers will be heard,
and that God's grace will be poured out
on all those who invoke you.

We approach your throne of mercy
with confidence, for we know
that those who come to you
with faith and love are never disappointed.
O Mary, Mother of God, and our mother,
pray for us, help us in our hour of need.
O Mary, take us up into heaven,
and plead for us.

    R. Amen.

Let us remember in these prayers all who are sick
and in need, our doctors, nurses, and caregivers, all our
relatives and friends, living and dead, and the souls of
all those recently deceased, as we seek the intercession
of the Holy Mother of God, and say together:

    R. Hail Mary, full of grace,
       the Lord is with thee.
       Blessed art thou among women
       and blessed is the fruit
       of thy womb Jesus.
       Holy Mary, Mother of God,
       pray for us sinners,
       now and at the hour of our death.
       Amen.

Prayer for the Evening

Those assembled make the sign of the cross, and the leader says this prayer.

O Lord,
when I lie down, I go to sleep in peace;
I am alone, O Lord; please keep me safe.
Thank you, O God, for this day,
for the love and patience
of all who have looked after me,
for laughter and smiles,
and the visitors who came to comfort.

O God, our Father,
give strength to the staff
who will be busy all night
caring for patients.
Calm those who will be restless,
and for whom the night will be long,
give comfort to those who are lonely.
O God, into your care I commit myself.
Help me to sleep each night, knowing your peace.
 R. *Amen.*

The leader concludes by saying to those present:

May the Lord be with you always,
to be your strength and your peace.
 R. *Thanks be to God.*

Triumph of the Cross

This feast is observed on September 14 and commemorates the victory that our Lord accomplished through his death and Resurrection. As a feast of Christ, when it falls on a Sunday, it replaces the liturgy for Ordinary Time.

Greeting

The leader offers a greeting to all present.

May the grace of our Lord Jesus Christ,
and the love of God,
and the fellowship of the Holy Spirit,
be with us all as we pray here together.
>   *R. Amen.*

Gathering Prayer

The leader begins by saying this opening prayer.

O Christ, you who became obedient even unto death on the cross, let us now praise and exalt you above all. May we venerate the wood, the nails, the crown, which are our salvation, and may this cross keep us from all harm.
>   *R. Amen.*

First Reading

The leader reads a passage from sacred Scripture. The theme of this text is God's power.

A reading from Paul's First Letter to the Corinthians 2:1–5

As for me, brothers, when I came to you, it was not with any show of oratory or philosophy, but simply to tell you what God had guaranteed. During my stay with you, the only knowledge I claimed to have was about Jesus, and only about him as the crucified Christ. Far from relying on any power of my own, I came among you in great "fear and trembling" and in the speeches and the sermons that I gave, there were none of the arguments that belong to philosophy; only a demonstration of the power of the Spirit. And I did this so that your faith would not depend on human philosophy but on the power of God.

R. The Word of the Lord.

Psalm 92:2–3, 5

The leader prays a brief psalm.

It is good to give thanks to the Lord,
to sing praise to your name, O Most High,
to proclaim your grace in the morning,
to declare your faithfulness at night....
For you make me glad with your deeds, O Lord,
and I sing for joy at the work of your hands.

Our Father

The leader introduces the Lord's Prayer.

We commend all whom we love, or who have been entrusted to our prayers, to the unfailing love of God, and say together, as Christ himself has taught us:

R. Our Father, who art in heaven,
hallowed be thy name;
thy kingdom come;
thy will be done
on earth as it is in heaven.
Give us this day our daily bread,
and forgive us our trespasses,
as we forgive those who trespass against us,
and lead us not into temptation,
but deliver us from evil.
Amen.

Second Reading

The leader reads this brief quotation.

Jesus is not violent; he is strong. His strength unmasks the real weakness hidden behind the physical violence of his enemies. Physical violence is a language of last resort, the language of weakness. When we slap a child, for example, that's when we admit that we have lost control of ourselves and the situation. We have lost the strength of gentleness.

PIERRE WOLFF

Prayer in the Midst of Illness

The leader shares this prayer with those present.

Father, your only Son took upon himself
the sufferings and weakness of all humankind;
through his passion and cross, he taught us
how good can be brought out of suffering.
Look upon our brothers and sisters who are ill.
In the midst of illness and pain,
may we be united with Christ,
who heals both body and soul,
and may we know the consolation promised
to those who suffer.
Through Christ our Lord.
  R. Amen.

Let us remember in these prayers all who are sick
and in need, our doctors, nurses, and caregivers, all our
relatives and friends, living and dead, and the souls of
all those recently deceased, as we seek the intercession
of the Holy Mother of God, and say together:

R. Hail Mary, full of grace,
the Lord is with thee.
Blessed art thou among women
and blessed is the fruit
of thy womb Jesus.
Holy Mary, Mother of God,
pray for us sinners,
now and at the hour of our death.
Amen.

John Henry Newman's Prayer for Peace

Those assembled make the sign of the cross, and the leader says this prayer.

May the Lord support us all the day long
till the shades lengthen
and the evening comes
and the busy world is hushed
and the fever of life is over
and our work is done.
Then in his mercy
may he give us a safe lodging
and a holy rest
and peace at the last.
　　R. Amen.

The leader concludes by saying to those present:

May the Lord be with you always,
to be your strength and your peace.
　　R. Thanks be to God.

Saint Francis of Assisi

Patron saint of Italy and of ecologists, as well as founder of the Franciscans, Francis of Assisi's feast day is celebrated on October 4.

Greeting

The leader offers a greeting to all present.

May the grace of our Lord Jesus Christ,
and the love of God,
and the fellowship of the Holy Spirit,
be with us all as we pray here together.
    R. Amen.

Gathering Prayer

The leader begins by saying this opening prayer.

O God, grant that we may imitate the humility, zeal, and wisdom of Saint Francis of Assisi, and grant that he may intercede for us on behalf of our intentions.
    R. Amen.

First Reading

The leader reads a passage from sacred Scripture. The theme of this text is hope in suffering.

A reading from the First Letter of Peter 3:14–17

If you have to suffer for being good, you will count it a blessing. There is no need to be afraid or to worry about persecutors. Simply reverence the Lord Christ in your hearts, and always have your answer ready for people who ask you the reason for the hope that you all have. But give it with courtesy and respect and with a clear conscience, so that those who slander you when you are living a good life in Christ, may be proved wrong in the accusations that they bring. And if it is the will of God that you should suffer, it is better to suffer for doing right than for doing wrong.

R. *The Word of the Lord.*

Psalm 41:2–4

The leader prays a brief psalm.

Blessed is he who regards the poor;
the Lord delivers him in time of trouble.
The Lord protects him, preserves his life,
and gives him happiness in the land....
The Lord helps him when he gets sick,
and heals him of all his ailments.

Our Father

The leader introduces the Lord's Prayer.

We commend all whom we love, or who have been entrusted to our prayers, to the unfailing love of God, and say together, as Christ himself has taught us:

> *R. Our Father, who art in heaven,*
> *hallowed be thy name;*
> *thy kingdom come;*
> *thy will be done*
> *on earth as it is in heaven.*
> *Give us this day our daily bread,*
> *and forgive us our trespasses,*
> *as we forgive those who trespass*
> *against us,*
> *and lead us not into temptation,*
> *but deliver us from evil.*
> *Amen.*

Second Reading

The leader reads this brief quotation.

When all the people had fallen silent and were standing reverently at attention, a flock of swallows, chattering and making a loud noise, were building nests in that same place. Since the blessed Saint Francis could not be heard by the people over the chattering of the birds, he spoke to them, saying: "My sisters, swallows, it is now time for me to speak, for you have already

spoken enough. Listen to the Word of the Lord, be silent and quiet until the Word of the Lord is finished."

THOMAS OF CELANO

Prayer to Follow the Example of Saint Francis

The leader shares this prayer with those present.

Lord God,
as you have taught your Church
that all the commandments are summed up
in the love of you and our neighbor,
grant that as we follow Saint Francis of Assisi,
we may be numbered among the blessed
in your kingdom.
We make our prayer through Christ our Lord.
    R. Amen.

Let us remember in these prayers all who are sick
and in need, our doctors, nurses, and caregivers, all our
relatives and friends, living and dead, and the souls of
all those recently deceased, as we seek the intercession
of the Holy Mother of God, and say together:

    R. Hail Mary, full of grace,
      the Lord is with thee.
      Blessed art thou among women
      and blessed is the fruit of thy womb Jesus.
      Holy Mary, Mother of God,
      pray for us sinners,
      now and at the hour of our death.
      Amen.

Prayer of Saint Francis of Assisi

Those assembled make the sign of the cross, and the leader says this prayer.

Lord, make me an instrument of your peace;
where there is hatred, let me sow love;
where there is injury, let me sow pardon;
where there is doubt, let me sow faith;
where there is despair, let me give hope;
where there is darkness, let me give light;
where there is sadness, let me give joy.
O Divine Master, grant that I may
not try to be comforted, but to understand;
not try to be loved, but to love,
because it is in giving that we receive,
it is in forgiving that we are forgiven,
and it is in dying that we are born to eternal life.
    R. *Amen.*

The leader concludes by saying to those present:

May the Lord be with you always,
to be your strength and your peace.
    R. *Thanks be to God.*

World Mission Sunday

Observed on the next-to-last Sunday in October, Pope John Paul II describes this celebration of the Church's missionary activity as an "important day...because it teaches how to give."

Greeting

The leader offers a greeting to all present.

May the grace of our Lord Jesus Christ,
and the love of God,
and the fellowship of the Holy Spirit,
be with us all as we pray here together.
    R. Amen.

Gathering Prayer

The leader begins by saying this opening prayer.

Father, may the faith for which the martyrs died spread throughout the world, and may all missionaries work to build up the Church at home and abroad. Finally may our lives be a missionary light to all the members of our community.
    R. Amen.

First Reading

The leader reads a passage from sacred Scripture. This text concerns baptism and repentance.

A reading from the Acts of the Apostles 2:14, 36–41

Then Peter stood up with the Eleven and addressed them in a loud voice: "The whole House of Israel can be certain that God has made this Jesus whom you crucified, both Lord and Christ."

Hearing this they were cut to the heart and said to Peter and the apostles, "What must we do, brothers?" "You must repent," Peter answered, "and every one of you must be baptized in the name of Jesus Christ for the forgiveness of your sins, and you will receive the gift of the Holy Spirit. The promise that was made is for you and your children, and for all those who are far away, for all those whom the Lord our God will call to himself."

He spoke to them for a long time using many arguments, and he urged them, "Save yourselves from this perverse generation."

They were convinced by his arguments, and they accepted what he said and were baptized. That very day, about three thousand were added to their number.

R. The Word of the Lord.

Psalm 8:2–3

The leader prays a brief psalm.

O Lord, our Lord,
how great is your name throughout the earth!
And your glory in the heavens above.
Even the mouths of children and infants
exalt your glory.

Our Father

The leader introduces the Lord's Prayer.

We commend all whom we love, or who have been entrusted to our prayers, to the unfailing love of God, and say together, as Christ himself has taught us:

> *R. Our Father, who art in heaven,*
> *hallowed be thy name;*
> *thy kingdom come;*
> *thy will be done*
> *on earth as it is in heaven.*
> *Give us this day our daily bread,*
> *and forgive us our trespasses,*
> *as we forgive those who trespass*
> *against us,*
> *and lead us not into temptation,*
> *but deliver us from evil.*
> *Amen.*

Second Reading

The leader reads this brief quotation.

Only Christianity remains standing today, able to measure up to the intellectual and moral world that exists in the West since the Renaissance....Christianity does not offer the opiate of a defeatist passivity, but the lucid rapture of a magnificent reality to be discovered by a push forward across the front of the Universe. Christianity has brought us up to this point. ...That is why it remains acceptable, as a belief, for a generation which does not ask of religion to only keep us wise, but to make us critical, enthusiastic seekers.

PIERRE TEILHARD DE CHARDIN

Prayer for Missionaries

The leader shares this prayer with those present.

We pray for all missionaries, that you sustain them when they are weary, lighten their hearts when they are sad, and help them to appreciate fully that it is you they are serving.

O Jesus, you suffered and died for us; you understand suffering.

Teach us to understand our suffering as you do: To bear it in union with you; To offer it with you to atone for our sins, and to bring your grace to souls in need. Calm our fears; increase our trust. May we gladly accept your holy will, and become more like you in trial.

So, my friends, be still and be comforted: The Lord

is with you, strengthening and supporting you. Put your trust in him for he loves and cares for you. Listen to Jesus when he says, "Peace, be still," and believe that he is with you, and will help you always.

R. *Amen.*

Let us remember in these prayers all who are sick and in need, our doctors, nurses, and caregivers, all our relatives and friends, living and dead, and the souls of all those recently deceased, as we seek the intercession of the Holy Mother of God, and say together:

R. *Hail Mary, full of grace,*
the Lord is with thee.
Blessed art thou among women
and blessed is the fruit
of thy womb Jesus.
Holy Mary, Mother of God,
pray for us sinners,
now and at the hour of our death.
Amen.

Prayer for Justice

Those assembled make the sign of the cross, and the leader says this prayer.

O God, our Father,
On the first Pentecost, you opened the hearts
of those who believed in you,
by the light of the Holy Spirit.

In the same Holy Spirit,
give us a desire for what is right and just,
and a continuing sense
of his presence and power in our lives.
We ask this through Christ our Lord.

> R. *Amen.*

The leader concludes by saying to those present:

May the Lord be with you always,
to be your strength and your peace.

> R. *Thanks be to God.*

Christ the King

This movable celebration is observed on the last Sunday of the liturgical year and commemorates the royal prerogatives of Christ.

Greeting

The leader offers a greeting to all present.

May the grace of our Lord Jesus Christ,
and the love of God,
and the fellowship of the Holy Spirit,
be with us all as we pray here together.
    R. Amen.

Gathering Prayer

The leader begins by saying this opening prayer.

Loving Father, you sent your Son to redeem us and cleanse us of our sins. He is our Lord and King because only he can bring us to holiness and happiness.
    R. Amen.

First Reading

The leader reads a passage from sacred Scripture. This text concerns the kingship of David.

All the tribes of Israel then came to David at Hebron. "Look," they said, "we are your own flesh and blood." In days past when Saul was our king, it was you who led Israel in all their exploits; and Yahweh said to you, "You are the man who shall be shepherd of my people Israel, you shall be the leader of Israel." So all the elders of Israel came to the king at Hebron, and King David made a pact with them at Hebron in the presence of Yahweh, and they anointed David King of Israel.

R. *The Word of the Lord.*

Psalm 71:1–4

The leader prays a brief psalm.

O God, endow the king with your justice,
the royal son with your righteousness.
May he rule your people justly
and defend the rights of the lowly.
Let the mountains bring peace to the people,
and the hills justice.
He will defend the cause of the poor,
deliver the children of the needy.

Our Father

The leader introduces the Lord's Prayer.

We commend all whom we love, or who have been entrusted to our prayers, to the unfailing love of God, and say together, as Christ himself has taught us:

R. *Our Father, who art in heaven,*
   hallowed be thy name;
   thy kingdom come;
   thy will be done on earth as it is in heaven.
   Give us this day our daily bread,
   and forgive us our trespasses,
   as we forgive those who trespass against us,
   and lead us not into temptation,
   but deliver us from evil.
   Amen.

Second Reading

The leader reads this brief quotation.

Listen to me on the Cathedral of the Cross, which I have placed in your heart so that I may live in you as a pilgrim, crucified in this world. You shall see me in your spirit, crucified on the bare cross of poverty, crucified in your body with the weakness of sickness, and crucified in your spirit through melancholy and weariness. And I shall bring this about in such a way that everything will be for you both a cross and a source of peace.

MOTHER MARIA CELESTE CROSTAROSA

Prayer of Comfort

The leader shares this prayer with those present.

Let us call ourselves to stillness—outer and inner,
close our eyes and relax the mind—
let our concerns just flow past,
knowing that God will take care of them—
just hand them over to him.

Lord Jesus, we thank you for your presence
in the heart of each of us,
and also as we gather together here
in *(give name of place)* to renew our faith.

We ask you to deepen our awareness of your love,
help us to respond as you offer to us your welcome,
as you offer your support to nourish us,
as you call us to your presence.

Let us pause for a moment
to recall an instance,
in each in our own lives
when your love has been especially clear to us—
a time when we were deeply aware of your support.

(Pause for reflection)

We thank you for that love
and also for all the times we have been
unaware of your care for us.

We ask too that we may in turn
be signs of your love to others
in the way that we cope with our own lives.
We ask this through Christ our Lord.
   R. Amen.

Let us remember in these prayers all who are sick
and in need, our doctors, nurses, and caregivers, all our
relatives and friends, living and dead, and the souls of
all those recently deceased, as we seek the intercession
of the Holy Mother of God, and say together:

> *R. Hail Mary, full of grace,*
> *the Lord is with thee.*
> *Blessed art thou among women*
> *and blessed is the fruit*
> *of thy womb Jesus.*
> *Holy Mary, Mother of God,*
> *pray for us sinners,*
> *now and at the hour of our death.*
> *Amen.*

Prayer for God's Care

*Those assembled make the sign of the cross, and the leader
says this prayer adapted from Psalm 121.*

I lift up my eyes to the hills:
Where is my help to come from?
My help comes from the Lord,
who has made both Heaven and earth.

He will not let you stumble or fall.
Your guardian will not sleep.
No—as the guardian of his people,
he never falls asleep

The Lord is your guardian,
he stays close at hand;
The sun will not strike you by day,
nor the moon by night.

The Lord will keep you from harm,
he watches over you.
The Lord watches over you as you come,
and as you go, now—and always.
    R. Amen.

The leader concludes by saying to those present:

May the Lord be with you always,
to be your strength and your peace.
    R. Thanks be to God.

All Saints

This solemn holy day of obligation is held on November 1 and commemorates all the blessed in heaven, particularly those who have no special feasts.

Greeting

The leader offers a greeting to all present.

May the grace of our Lord Jesus Christ,
and the love of God,
and the fellowship of the Holy Spirit,
be with us all as we pray here together.
    R. Amen.

Gathering Prayer

The leader begins by saying this opening prayer.

Almighty and eternal God who has gathered all his saints to himself, grant that through the intercession of these multitudes our pleas may be heard and heeded.
    R. Amen.

First Reading

The leader reads a passage from sacred Scripture. This text gives the Beatitudes.

A reading from the Gospel according to
Matthew 5:1–12

Seeing the crowds, Jesus went up the hill. There he sat down and was joined by his disciples. Then he began to speak. This is what he taught them:

"How happy are the poor in spirit,
theirs is the kingdom of heaven.
Happy the gentle:
they shall have the earth for their heritage.
Happy those who mourn:
they shall be comforted.
Happy those who hunger and thirst for what is right;
they shall be satisfied.
Happy the merciful;
they shall have mercy shown them.
Happy the pure in heart;
they shall see God.
Happy the peacemakers;
they shall be called children of God.
Happy are those who are persecuted
in the cause of right;
theirs is the kingdom of heaven.

Happy are you when people abuse you and persecute you and speak all kinds of calumny against you on my account. Rejoice and be glad, for your reward will be great in heaven; this is how they persecuted the prophets before you.

R. The Gospel of the Lord.

Psalm 36:6–8

The leader prays a brief psalm.

Your love, O God, reaches the heavens;
your faithfulness, to the clouds.
Your justice is like the mighty mountains;
your judgment like the unfathomable deep.
You preserve, O Lord, humans and beasts.
How precious, O God, is your constant love!
Humans take refuge in the shadow of your wings.

Our Father

The leader introduces the Lord's Prayer.

We commend all whom we love, or who have been
entrusted to our prayers, to the unfailing love of God,
and say together, as Christ himself has taught us:

> R. *Our Father, who art in heaven,*
> *hallowed be thy name;*
> *thy kingdom come;*
> *thy will be done*
> *on earth as it is in heaven.*
> *Give us this day our daily bread,*
> *and forgive us our trespasses,*
> *as we forgive those who trespass*
> *against us,*
> *and lead us not into temptation,*
> *but deliver us from evil.*
> *Amen.*

Second Reading

The leader reads this brief quotation.

When an apprentice gets hurt, or complains of
being tired, the women and peasants have this fine ex-
pression: "It is the trade entering his body." Each time
that we have some pain to go through, we can say to
ourselves quite truly that it is the universe, the order
and beauty of the world, and the obedience of God
that are entering our body.

SIMONE WEIL

Prayer for Patience

The leader shares this prayer with those present.

Father, your Son accepted his sufferings
in order to show us the virtue
of patience in the face of human illness.
Hear the prayers we offer
for our sick brothers and sisters.
May all who suffer pain, illness, or disease
realize that they are chosen to be saints,
and know that they are joined to Christ
in his sufferings for the salvation of the world,
who lives and reigns for ever.
　　R. Amen.

Let us remember in these prayers all who are sick
and in need, our doctors, nurses, and caregivers, all our
relatives and friends, living and dead, and the souls of

all those recently deceased, as we seek the intercession
of the Holy Mother of God, and say together:

> R. *Hail Mary, full of grace,*
> *the Lord is with thee.*
> *Blessed art thou among women*
> *and blessed is the fruit of thy womb Jesus.*
> *Holy Mary, Mother of God,*
> *pray for us sinners,*
> *now and at the hour of our death.*
> *Amen.*

Prayer for Trust in God

Making the sign of the cross, the leader says this prayer.

Cheer up, God is with you.
You suffer, it is true, but he is near you.
Trust in him
as you would trust in your own father.
If he has let you suffer,
it is because he sees something good in it,
which today you do not yet know.
Your peace of mind is in your trust in God
who can never let you down.

> R. *Amen.*

The leader concludes by saying to those present:

May the Lord be with you always,
to be your strength and your peace.

> R. *Thanks be to God.*

All Souls

This commemoration of the Faithful Departed is held on November 2.

Greeting

The leader offers a greeting to all present.

May the grace of our Lord Jesus Christ,
and the love of God,
and the fellowship of the Holy Spirit,
be with us all as we pray here together.
> **R.** *Amen.*

Gathering Prayer

The leader begins by saying this opening prayer.

O God, our creator and redeemer, who in the death of your only Son gave us life, have mercy on all those who have died. Lead them into the Promised Land of heaven.
> **R.** *Amen.*

First Reading

The leader reads a passage from sacred Scripture. This text concerns God's mercy.

A reading from the First Letter of Peter 1:3–9

Blessed be God the Father of our Lord Jesus Christ, who in his great mercy has given us a new birth as his sons, by raising Jesus Christ from the dead, so that we have a sure hope and the promise of an inheritance that can never be spoiled or soiled and never fade away, because it is being kept for you in the heavens. Through your faith, God's power will guard you until the salvation which has been prepared is revealed at the end of time.

This is a cause of great joy for you, even though you may for a short time have to bear being plagued by all sorts of trials; so that, when Jesus Christ is revealed, your faith will have been tested and proved like gold—only it is more precious than gold, which is corruptible even though it bears testing by fire—and then you will have praise and glory and honor.

You did not see him, yet you love him; and still without seeing him, you are already filled with a joy so glorious that it cannot be described, because you believe; and you are sure of the end to which your faith looks forward, that is, the salvation of your souls.

R. The Word of the Lord.

Psalm 66:3–4

The leader prays a brief psalm.

All mortals bring to you their evil deeds,
to you, who answers prayers.
Though our faults prevail over us,
you forgive our sins.

Our Father

The leader introduces the Lord's Prayer.

We commend all whom we love, or who have been entrusted to our prayers, to the unfailing love of God, and say together, as Christ himself has taught us:

R. Our Father, who art in heaven,
hallowed be thy name;
thy kingdom come;
thy will be done
on earth as it is in heaven.
Give us this day our daily bread,
and forgive us our trespasses
as we forgive those who trespass
against us,
and lead us not into temptation,
but deliver us from evil.
Amen.

Second Reading

The leader reads this brief quotation.

Remember that you have only one death to die; that you have only one life, which is short and has to be lived by you alone; and there is only one glory, which is eternal. If you do this, there will be many things about which you care nothing.

SAINT TERESA OF ÁVILA

Prayer for All Souls

The leader shares this prayer with those present.

Father, hear the prayers
of the family you have gathered before you.
In mercy and love,
unite all your children wherever they may be.
Welcome into your kingdom
our departed brothers and sisters,
and all who have left this world
in your friendship.
There we hope to share in your glory
when every tear will be wiped away.
On that day we shall see you,
our God, as you are.
We shall become like you
and praise you forever.
Through Christ our Lord,
from whom all good things come.
  R. Amen.

Let us remember in these prayers all who are sick
and in need, our doctors, nurses, and caregivers, all our
relatives and friends, living and dead, and the souls of
all those recently deceased, as we seek the intercession
of the Holy Mother of God, and say together:

*R. Hail Mary, full of grace,
the Lord is with thee.
Blessed art thou among women
and blessed is the fruit of thy womb Jesus.*

Holy Mary, Mother of God,
pray for us sinners,
now and at the hour of our death.
Amen.

Prayer for Reassurance in Suffering

Those assembled make the sign of the cross, and the leader
says this final prayer.

My brothers and sisters, remember,
you will have to suffer only for a little while.
The God of all grace will see that all is well again.
He will confirm, strengthen, and support you.
His power lasts forever and ever.
    R. *Amen.*

The leader concludes by saying to those present:

May the Lord be with you always,
to be your strength and your peace.
    R. *Thanks be to God.*

Ordinary Time No. 1

Ordinary Time is the name given to the thirty-three or thirty-four weeks of the liturgical year which elaborate the themes of salvation history. The first segment of Ordinary Time begins on the Monday (or Tuesday if the feast of the Baptism of the Lord is celebrated on that Monday) after the Sunday following January 6 and continues until and including Shrove Tuesday. It then resumes on the Monday after Pentecost and continues until the first Sunday of Advent.

Greeting

The leader offers a greeting to all present.

May the grace of our Lord Jesus Christ,
and the love of God,
and the fellowship of the Holy Spirit,
be with us all as we pray here together.
   R. Amen.

Gathering Prayer

The leader begins by saying this opening prayer.

Generous Father, grant us the means necessary to follow you faithfully and obtain the good things which you promise.
   R. Amen.

First Reading

The leader reads a passage from sacred Scripture. In this text, Christ declares that he is the "living bread."

A reading from the Gospel according to John 6:51

Jesus says:
"I am the living bread
which has come down from heaven.
Anyone who eats this bread will live for ever;
and the bread that I shall give is my flesh,
for the life of the world."
    R. *The Gospel of the Lord.*

Psalm 65:12–13

The leader prays a brief psalm.

You crown the year with your goodness;
abundance flows everywhere.
The deserts have become pasture land,
the hills are clothed with gladness.

Our Father

The leader introduces the Lord's Prayer.

    We commend all whom we love, or who have been entrusted to our prayers, to the unfailing love of God, and say together, as Christ himself has taught us:

R. Our Father, who art in heaven,
   hallowed be thy name;
   thy kingdom come;
   thy will be done
   on earth as it is in heaven.
   Give us this day our daily bread,
   and forgive us our trespasses,
   as we forgive those who trespass
   against us,
   and lead us not into temptation,
   but deliver us from evil.
   Amen.

Second Reading

The leader reads this brief quotation.

When Jesus says, "Blessed are you poor; the reign of God is yours," it is not because poverty is blessed but because he is, himself, a blessing. The reign he is talking about is the one established by a king according to God's heart: a liberator of his people, against external enemies, of course, but also by justice toward the lowly within the kingdom.

PIERRE WOLFF

Prayer of Thanksgiving

The leader shares this prayer with those present. It has been adapted from Psalm 138.

Lord, with all my heart I thank you.
I bow down and praise your name,
because of your constant love and faithfulness.
You created every part of me.
You put me together in my mother's womb
and when I was growing in secret,
you knew I was there.
You saw me before I was born,
and planned every day of my life
before I began to breathe.
Every day was recorded in your book.

How precious it is, Lord, to realize
that you are thinking constantly about me.
I can't even count how many times a day
your thoughts turn towards me,
and when after sleep I wake in the morning
you're still thinking of me.
When I pray you answer me and encourage me
by giving me the strength I need.
Lord, with all my heart,
I thank you for all your goodness to me.
  R. Amen.

Let us remember in these prayers all who are sick
and in need, our doctors, nurses, and caregivers, all our
relatives and friends, living and dead, and the souls of
all those recently deceased, as we seek the intercession
of the Holy Mother of God, and say together:

R. Hail Mary, full of grace,
the Lord is with thee.
Blessed art thou among women
and blessed is the fruit
of thy womb Jesus.
Holy Mary, Mother of God,
pray for us sinners,
now and at the hour of our death.
Amen.

Prayer of Thanksgiving

Those assembled make the sign of the cross, and the leader says this final prayer.

My God, from my heart I thank you for the many
blessings you have given to me.
I thank you for having created and baptized me,
and for having placed me in your
holy Catholic Church;
and for having given me so many graces and mercies
through the merit of Jesus Christ.
And I thank you, dear Jesus,
for having become a little child for my sake,
to teach me to be holy and humble like you;
and for having died upon the cross
that I might have pardon for my sins
and get to heaven.
Also, I thank you for all your other mercies,
most of all for those you have given me today.

R. Amen.

The leader concludes by saying to those present:

May the Lord be with you always,
to be your strength and your peace.
R. *Thanks be to God.*

Ordinary Time No. 2

Greeting

The leader offers a greeting to all present.

May the grace of our Lord Jesus Christ,
and the love of God,
and the fellowship of the Holy Spirit,
be with us all as we pray here together.
  R. Amen.

Gathering Prayer

The leader begins by saying this opening prayer.

All-seeing Father, help us live a life according to your will, so that we may bear abundant good works in your name and that of your Son, Jesus Christ, who lives and reigns with you.
  R. Amen.

First Reading

The leader reads a passage from sacred Scripture. This text concerns faith.

A reading from the First Letter of Paul to the Corinthians 15:1–8

Brothers, I want to remind you of the gospel I preached to you, the gospel that you received and in which you are firmly established; because the gospel will save you only if you keep believing exactly what I preached to you—believing anything else will not lead to anything.

Well then, in the first place, I taught you what I had been taught myself, namely that Christ died for our sins, in accordance with the scriptures; that he was buried; and that he was raised to life on the third day, in accordance with the scriptures; that he appeared first to Cephas and secondly to the Twelve. Next, he appeared to more than five hundred of the brothers at the same time, most of whom are still alive, though some have died; then he appeared to James, and then to all the apostles; and last of all he appeared to me too; it was as though I was born when no one expected it.

R. *The Word of the Lord.*

Psalm 71:20–21

The leader prays a brief psalm.

Many have been my hardships and misery,
but once more you come to revive me;
from the depths of the earth
you will bring me up again.
You will restore me and comfort me again.

Our Father

The leader introduces the Lord's Prayer.

We commend all whom we love, or who have been entrusted to our prayers, to the unfailing love of God, and say together, as Christ himself has taught us:

R. *Our Father, who art in heaven,*
hallowed be thy name;
thy kingdom come;
thy will be done on earth as it is in heaven.
Give us this day our daily bread,
and forgive us our trespasses,
as we forgive those who trespass against us,
and lead us not into temptation,
but deliver us from evil.
Amen.

Second Reading

The leader reads this brief quotation.

Saint Teresa of Ávila recommended this exercise to everybody: "Imagine you see Jesus standing before you….He is looking at you….Notice him looking at you." She adds two very important adverbs, however. *Notice him looking at you,* she says, *lovingly and humbly.* See him look at you with love; see him look at you with humility.

Many find it hard to imagine Jesus looking at them lovingly—their image of Jesus is the image of someone who is harsh and demanding, someone who loves them only if they are good. The second attitude they find even more difficult to accept. That Jesus should look at them humbly....Once again, they have not taken seriously that fact that Jesus has become their servant and slave, the one who willingly died the death of a slave out of love for them.

ANTHONY DE MELLO

Prayer in the Face of Sickness

The leader shares this prayer with those present.

My God, you have created me for your purpose,
I know I have my place in your plan.
I may never know what it is in this life,
but I will be told it in the next.
So I will trust you in all things.
If I am sick, may my sickness serve you.
If I am worried, may my worry serve you.
If I am in sorrow, may my sorrow serve you.
If I am exhausted, may my exhaustion serve you.
If I am sleepless, may my wakefulness serve you.
    R. Amen.

Let us remember in these prayers all who are sick and in need, our doctors, nurses, and caregivers, all our relatives and friends, living and dead, and the souls of all those recently deceased, as we seek the intercession of the Holy Mother of God, and say together:

R. *Hail Mary, full of grace,*
   the Lord is with thee.
   Blessed art thou among women
   and blessed is the fruit
   of thy womb Jesus.
   Holy Mary, Mother of God,
   pray for us sinners,
   now and at the hour of our death.
   Amen.

Prayer of Thanksgiving for the Eucharist

Those assembled make the sign of the cross, and the leader says this prayer.

I give you thanks,
Lord, Holy Father, everlasting God.
In your great mercy,
and not because of my own merits,
you have fed me, an unworthy sinner,
with the precious Body and Blood of your Son,
our Lord Jesus Christ.

May it be my armor of faith
and shield of good purpose.
May it root out in me all vice and evil desires,
increase my love and patience,
humility and obedience,
and every virtue.

Make it a firm defense
against the wiles of all my enemies,
while restraining all evil impulses
of flesh and spirit.
May it help me to cling to you,
the one true God,
and bring me a blessed death when you call.

I beseech you to bring me, a sinner,
to that glorious feast where,
with your Son and Holy Spirit,
you are the true light of your holy ones,
their flawless blessedness,
everlasting joy,
and perfect happiness.
Through Christ our Lord.
    R. Amen.

The leader concludes by saying to those present:

May the Lord be with you always,
to be your strength and your peace.
    R. Thanks be to God.

Ordinary Time No. 3

This prayer service may be used for optional dates within Ordinary Time.

Greeting

The leader offers a greeting to all present.

May the grace of our Lord Jesus Christ,
and the love of God,
and the fellowship of the Holy Spirit,
be with us all as we pray here together.
    R. Amen.

Gathering Prayer

The leader begins by saying this opening prayer.

Lord, watch over us with your constant love; protect and defend us always since we put our hope in you alone. Through Christ our Lord.
    R. Amen.

First Reading

The leader reads a passage from sacred Scripture. This text concerns the easy "yoke" of our Lord.

A reading from the Gospel of Matthew 11:28–30

Come to me, all you who labor and are overburdened, and I will give you rest. Shoulder my yoke and learn from me, for I am gentle and humble in heart, and you will find rest for your souls. Yes, my yoke is easy and my burden light.

R. *The Gospel of the Lord.*

Psalm 117:17–18

The leader prays a brief psalm.

I shall not die, but live
to proclaim what the Lord has done.
The Lord has stricken me severely,
but he has saved me from death.

Our Father

The leader introduces the Lord's Prayer.

We commend all whom we love, or who have been entrusted to our prayers, to the unfailing love of God, and say together, as Christ himself has taught us:

R. *Our Father, who art in heaven,*
  hallowed be thy name;
  thy kingdom come;
  thy will be done on earth as it is in heaven.
  Give us this day our daily bread,
  and forgive us our trespasses,

as we forgive those who trespass against us,
and lead us not into temptation,
but deliver us from evil.
Amen.

Second Reading

The leader reads this brief quotation.

For you who live after Jesus and believe in him, the old world has ceased. You have seen through the deceit and vanity of the old world; it has no staying power, no substance. For this reason, you are not to trust it nor be afraid of it....You are safe in every unrest. The sufferings of all have been carried by Jesus to the Father. Therefore, you can no longer speak of the tragedy of life. Tragedy has been turned into a saving cross.

WILFRID STINISSEN, O. CARM.

Prayer to Alleviate Isolation

The leader shares this prayer with those present.

Lord Jesus,
you entered our world and shared our condition,
bring health to the sick,
and give the dying a share in your glory.
In this place, Jesus, there are some who are suffering,
and some very isolated in their pain.

Give us your love in answer to these prayers,
And help us to bear our cross of anxiety and sickness.
Strengthen our faith
so that we may help those around us
who do not know or love you.
Lord, we believe in you and your love for us,
Increase our faith and trust.

R. *Amen.*

Let us remember in these prayers all who are sick and in need, our doctors, nurses, and caregivers, all our relatives and friends, living and dead, and the souls of all those recently deceased, as we seek the intercession of the Holy Mother of God, and say together:

R. *Hail Mary, full of grace,*
the Lord is with thee.
Blessed art thou among women
and blessed is the fruit
of thy womb Jesus.
Holy Mary, Mother of God,
pray for us sinners,
now and at the hour of our death.
Amen.

Prayer for God's Healing Care

Those assembled make the sign of the cross, and the leader says this prayer.

God is with you now,
nothing is more certain than that.
Throughout his life Jesus loved people
so deeply and completely that they were healed
of whatever was destroying them,
whether that was physical or mental illness,
or emotional or spiritual suffering.
That is what he continues to do.

In our growing closeness to Christ,
we receive a new vision of life,
a vision that sees everything
in the light of God's eternal love.
This love is lasting; no sickness is final,
and even death cannot withstand such love.
When we are anointed with oil,
a symbol of healing in Christ's time,
we receive a sign of Christ's healing care.
It is only his strength that can lift us out
of our present suffering, to joy and to peace.
    R. Amen.

The leader concludes by saying to those present:

May the Lord be with you always,
to be your strength and your peace.
    R. Thanks be to God.

Ordinary Time No. 4

This prayer service may be used for optional dates during Ordinary Time.

Greeting

The leader offers a greeting to all present.

May the grace of our Lord Jesus Christ,
and the love of God,
and the fellowship of the Holy Spirit,
be with us all as we pray here together.
    R. Amen.

Gathering Prayer

The leader begins by saying this opening prayer.

    Lord, you are pleased to dwell in those who are pure and sincere in heart. Grant that we may live our lives in a way that is always worthy of your company. Through Christ, our Lord.
    R. Amen.

First Reading

The leader reads a passage from sacred Scripture. The theme of this text is God's consolation in suffering.

A reading from the Second Letter of Paul to the Corinthians 1:3–7

Blessed be the God and Father of our Lord Jesus Christ, a gentle Father and the God of all consolation, who comforts us in all our sorrows, so that we can offer others, in their sorrows, the consolation that we ourselves have received from God.

Indeed, as the sufferings of Christ overflow to us, so, through Christ, does our consolation overflow. When we are able to suffer, it is for your consolation and salvation. When, instead, we are comforted, this should be a consolation to you, supporting you in patiently bearing the same sufferings as we bear. And our hope for you is confident, since we know that in sharing our sufferings, you will also share our consolations.

R. The Word of the Lord.

Psalm 6:8–10

The leader prays a brief psalm.

My eyes have grown dim from troubles;
I have weakened because of my foes.
Away from me, you evildoers,
for the Lord has heard my plaintive voice.
The Lord has heard my plea;
the Lord will grant all that I pray for.

Our Father

The leader introduces the Lord's Prayer.

We commend all whom we love, or who have been entrusted to our prayers, to the unfailing love of God, and say together, as Christ himself has taught us:

R. *Our Father, who art in heaven,*
   hallowed be thy name;
   thy kingdom come;
   thy will be done
   on earth as it is in heaven.
   Give us this day our daily bread,
   and forgive us our trespasses,
   as we forgive those who trespass
   against us,
   and lead us not into temptation,
   but deliver us from evil.
   Amen.

Second Reading

The leader reads this brief quotation.

A headache, work, dryness of spirit, fatigue. There was a time when faced with such obstacles, I would say: "When they are all over, I will begin to live again." Now I understand otherwise: the moment to live is always the present moment. It is the only way to be united with God.

MOTHER GENEVIEVE GALLOIS

Prayer for Emotional Healing

The leader shares this prayer with those present.

Father, may your gifts from heaven
free our hearts to serve you.
May the prayers we offer this day
bring us comfort and healing,
and lead us to eternal glory
where Jesus is Lord forever and ever.
We make our prayer through Christ our Lord.
  R. Amen.

Let us remember in these prayers all who are sick
and in need, our doctors, nurses, and caregivers, all our
relatives and friends, living and dead, and the souls of
all those recently deceased, as we seek the intercession
of the Holy Mother of God, and say together:

  R. Hail Mary, full of grace,
  the Lord is with thee.
  Blessed art thou among women
  and blessed is the fruit
  of thy womb Jesus.
  Holy Mary, Mother of God,
  pray for us sinners,
  now and at the hour of our death.
  Amen.

Prayer for the Blind

*Those assembled make the sign of the cross, and the leader
says this prayer.*

Almighty God, the fountain of all wisdom,
you know our needs before we ask,
and our ignorance in asking.
We beseech you
to have compassion on our plight,
and grant things for which we are unworthy to ask,
and for those of us blind,
vouchsafe to grant us your mercy,
Through Jesus Christ our Lord.
    R. Amen.

The leader concludes by saying to those present:

May the Lord be with you always,
to be your strength and your peace.
    R. Thanks be to God.

Ordinary Time No. 5

This prayer service may be used for optional dates during Ordinary Time.

Greeting

The leader offers a greeting to all present.

May the grace of our Lord Jesus Christ,
and the love of God,
and the fellowship of the Holy Spirit,
be with us all as we pray here together.
    R. *Amen.*

Gathering Prayer

The leader begins by saying this opening prayer.

Lord, we trust in your providence, which never fails; and grant us those blessings that may help us in our present and our future lives. Through Christ our Lord.
    R. *Amen.*

First Reading

The leader reads a passage from sacred Scripture. This text reminds us that heaven is our ultimate home.

A reading from the Letter of Paul to the Philippians 3:20—4:1

For us, our homeland is in heaven, and from heaven comes the Savior we are waiting for, the Lord Jesus Christ, and he will transfigure these wretched bodies of ours into copies of his glorious Body. He will do that by the same power with which he can subdue the whole universe. So then, my brothers and dear friends, do not give way but remain faithful in the Lord.

R. The Word of the Lord.

Psalm 9:10–11

The leader prays a brief psalm.

The Lord is a rampart for the oppressed,
a refuge in times of distress.
Those who cherish your name, O Lord,
can rely on you,
for you have never forsaken those who look to you.

Our Father

The leader introduces the Lord's Prayer.

We commend all whom we love, or who have been entrusted to our prayers, to the unfailing love of God, and say together, as Christ himself has taught us:

R. Our Father, who art in heaven,
hallowed be thy name;
thy kingdom come;

thy will be done
on earth as it is in heaven.
Give us this day our daily bread,
and forgive us our trespasses,
as we forgive those who trespass
against us,
and lead us not into temptation,
but deliver us from evil.
Amen.

Second Reading

The leader reads this brief quotation.

Think how small the little foot of Our Lord was on that first Christmas. A little foot does not make big strides; it can only take little steps. In imitating the Divine Babe, let us place our feet in His footsteps. Then we shall, with God's grace, grow into the bigger foot-steps and make greater strides. If we are faithful in little, we will obtain grace for the big.

SAINT KATHARINE DREXEL

Prayer to Our Lady

The leader shares this prayer with those present.

Remember, O most gracious virgin Mary,
that never was it known,
that anyone who fled to your protection,
implored your help,
or sought your intercession was left unaided.

Inspired with this confidence,
we fly unto you,
O Virgin of Virgins, our Mother.
To you we come, before you we stand,
sinful and sorrowful.
O Mother of the Word Incarnate,
despise not our petitions,
but in your mercy hear and answer us.
> *R. Amen.*

Let us remember in these prayers all who are sick and in need, our doctors, nurses, and caregivers, all our relatives and friends, living and dead, and the souls of all those recently deceased, as we seek the intercession of the Holy Mother of God, and say together:

> *R. Hail Mary, full of grace,*
> *the Lord is with thee.*
> *Blessed art thou among women*
> *and blessed is the fruit*
> *of thy womb Jesus.*
> *Holy Mary, Mother of God,*
> *pray for us sinners,*
> *now and at the hour of our death.*
> *Amen.*

A Journey to Night Prayers at Lourdes

Those assembled make the sign of the cross, and the leader presents this reflection.

Together the throng strolls arm in arm
through the meadow gate
over pastures green by day
but dark so late.

Over the bridge the water flowing
fast beneath us in the night,
the ripples dancing
in the Grotto light.

Hundreds of candles all aglow,
delivering prayers for people we know.
Soon silently we sit in prayer
Beneath Our Lady's compassionate stare.

We are but specks in the universe
trying to make sense as we traverse.
Endlessly seeking better things,
but it's love and prayer that peace brings.

So in the glow of the Grotto on this night,
we refurbish our souls and strengthen our might.
Then together we return to the meadow gate,
the stars above and the hour so late.

A PILGRIM TO LOURDES

The leader concludes by saying to those present:

May the Lord be with you always,
to be your strength and your peace.
    R. *Thanks be to God.*

Ordinary Time No. 6

This prayer service may be used for optional dates during Ordinary Time.

Greeting

The leader offers a greeting to all present.

May the grace of our Lord Jesus Christ,
and the love of God,
and the fellowship of the Holy Spirit,
be with us all as we pray here together.
R. *Amen.*

Gathering Prayer

The leader begins by saying this opening prayer.

O God of Strength, we hope in you, hear our prayer. Since we are weak and can do nothing without you, grant us your help in all that we do. Through Christ our Lord.
R. *Amen.*

First Reading

The leader reads a passage from sacred Scripture. This text concerns faith and love.

A reading from the First Letter of John 4:16

We ourselves have known and put our faith
in God's love towards ourselves.
God is love,
and anyone who lives in love lives in God,
and God lives in him.
> R. *The Word of the Lord.*

Psalm 16:9–11
The leader prays a brief psalm.

My soul rejoices;
my body too will rest assured.
For you will not abandon
my soul to the grave....
You will show me the path of life,
in your presence is the fullness of joy,
at your right hand is happiness forever.

Our Father
The leader introduces the Lord's Prayer.

We commend all whom we love, or who have been
entrusted to our prayers, to the unfailing love of God,
and say together, as Christ himself has taught us:

> R. *Our Father, who art in heaven,*
> *hallowed be thy name;*
> *thy kingdom come;*
> *thy will be done on earth as it is in heaven.*

Give us this day our daily bread,
and forgive us our trespasses,
as we forgive those who trespass against us,
and lead us not into temptation,
but deliver us from evil.
Amen.

Second Reading

The leader reads this brief quotation.

True devotion [living the path of sainthood]... perfects all things....Care of one's family is rendered more peaceable, love of husband and wife more sincere, service to the State more faithful and every type of employment more pleasant and agreeable.

SAINT FRANCIS DE SALES

Prayer for Comfort

The leader shares this prayer with those present.

Father,
We rejoice in the privilege
which enabled Our Lady
to be the Mother of God.
Grant that through her prayers,
we may come to you cleansed from sin.
Through the prayers of Mary, our mother,
heal the sick, comfort the suffering, pardon sinners,
and grant peace and salvation to us all.
R. Amen.

Let us remember in these prayers all who are sick and in need, our doctors, nurses, and caregivers, all our relatives and friends, living and dead, and the souls of all those recently deceased, as we seek the intercession of the Holy Mother of God, and say together:

R. *Hail Mary, full of grace,*
the Lord is with thee.
Blessed art thou among women
and blessed is the fruit of thy womb Jesus.
Holy Mary, Mother of God,
pray for us sinners,
now and at the hour of our death.
Amen.

Prayer for Help in Healing

Those assembled make the sign of the cross, and the leader says this prayer.

O God,
give us faith and patience,
we humbly ask of you.
May our prayers help us
to gain a deeper belief
in your healing-help.
May we bear the sufferings of this life
without wavering;
and come with joy to the presence of heaven.
We ask this through Christ our Lord.

R. *Amen.*

The leader concludes by saying to those present:

May the Lord be with you always,
to be your strength and your peace.
    R. *Thanks be to God.*

Service for the Seriously Ill

This prayer service may be used on optional dates during Ordinary Time or at other times as a service for the seriously ill.

Greeting

The leader offers a greeting to all present.

May the grace of our Lord Jesus Christ,
and the love of God,
and the fellowship of the Holy Spirit,
be with us all as we pray here together.
   R. Amen.

Gathering Prayer

The leader begins by saying this opening prayer.

   Almighty God, who has given us the gift of salvation and the promise of eternal life, look mercifully on us and in the hour of our going forth may we be found without stain of sin. Through Christ our Lord.
   R. Amen.

First Reading

The leader reads a passage from sacred Scripture. This text concerns our Final Judgment before God and points out that alive or dead we belong to the Lord.

A reading from Paul's Letter to the Romans 14:7–9, 11–12

The life and death of each of us has its influence on others; if we live, we live for the Lord; and if we die, we die for the Lord, so that alive or dead we belong to the Lord. This explains why Christ both died and came to life, it was so that he might be Lord both of the dead and of the living....We shall all have to stand before the judgment seat of God; as scripture says: By my life— it is the Lord who speaks—every knee shall bend before me, and every tongue shall praise God. It is to God, therefore, that each of us must give an account of himself.

R. The Word of the Lord.

Psalm 23:4

The leader prays a brief psalm.

Although I walk through the valley
of the shadow of death,
I fear no evil,
for you are beside me.

Our Father

The leader introduces the Lord's Prayer.

We commend all whom we love, or who have been entrusted to our prayers, to the unfailing love of God, and say together, as Christ himself has taught us:

R. *Our Father, who art in heaven,*
hallowed be thy name;
thy kingdom come;
thy will be done
on earth as it is in heaven.
Give us this day our daily bread,
and forgive us our trespasses
as we forgive those who trespass
against us,
and lead us not into temptation,
but deliver us from evil.
Amen.

Second Reading

The leader reads this brief quotation.

I never thank God for loving me, he can't avoid it, whether he wants to or not, his nature forces him to. I thank him rather that, in his bounty, he can't stop himself from loving me.

MEISTER ECKHART

Prayer for the Seriously Ill

The leader shares this prayer with those present.

Behold me, my beloved Jesus; weighed down under the burden of my trials and sufferings, I cast myself at your feet, that you may renew my strength and my courage, while I rest here in your presence.

Permit me to lay down my cross in your Sacred Heart, for only your infinite goodness can sustain me; only your love can help me bear my cross; only your powerful hand can lighten its weight.

O Divine King, Jesus, whose heart is so compassionate to the afflicted. I wish to live in you; suffer and die in you. During my life, be to me my model and my support; at the hour of my death, be my hope and my refuge.

R. Amen.

Let us remember in these prayers all who are sick and in need, our doctors, nurses, and caregivers, all our relatives and friends, living and dead, and the souls of all those recently deceased, as we seek the intercession of the Holy Mother of God, and say together:

R. Hail Mary, full of grace,
the Lord is with thee.
Blessed art thou among women
and blessed is the fruit of thy womb Jesus.
Holy Mary, Mother of God,
pray for us sinners,
now and at the hour of our death.
Amen.

Prayer for True Health

Those assembled make the sign of the cross, and the leader says this final prayer.

Lord, you are the source of eternal health
for those who believe in you.
May our brothers and sisters
who have been refreshed with these prayers,
together with all who believe in God's love,
safely reach your Kingdom of light,
life and peace, as we all seek to do.
We ask this through our Lord Jesus Christ.
R. *Amen.*

The leader concludes by saying to those present:

May the Lord be with you always,
to be your strength and your peace.
R. *Thanks be to God.*

Service for the Disabled

This prayer service may be used on optional dates during Ordinary Time or as a special service for the disabled.

Greeting

The leader offers a greeting to all present.

May the grace of our Lord Jesus Christ,
and the love of God,
and the fellowship of the Holy Spirit,
be with us all as we pray here together.
　　R. Amen.

Gathering Prayer

The leader begins by saying this opening prayer.

O God, who knows the secrets of every heart, purify us by the grace of the Holy Spirit so that we may give you worthy praise. Through Christ our Lord.
　　R. Amen.

First Reading

The leader reads a passage from sacred Scripture. This text concerns God's love for us.

*A reading from the Gospel according to
John 15:12–17*

Jesus said to his disciples:
This is my commandment:
love one another,
as I have loved you.
A man can have no greater love
than to lay down his life for his friends.
You are my friends,
if you do what I command you.
I shall not call you servants any more,
because a servant does not know
his master's business;
I call you friends,
because I have made known to you
everything I have learned from my Father.
You did not choose me,
no, I chose you;
and I commissioned you
to go out and to bear fruit,
fruit that will last;
and then the Father will give you
anything you ask him in my name.
What I command you
is to love one another.
R. *The Gospel of the Lord.*

Psalm 66:2

The leader prays a brief psalm.

May God be gracious and bless us;
may he let his face shine upon us,
that your way be known on earth
and your salvation among the nations.

Our Father

The leader introduces the Lord's Prayer.

We commend all whom we love, or who have been
entrusted to our prayers, to the unfailing love of God,
and say together, as Christ himself has taught us:

> *R. Our Father, who art in heaven,*
> *hallowed be thy name;*
> *thy kingdom come;*
> *thy will be done*
> *on earth as it is in heaven.*
> *Give us this day our daily bread,*
> *and forgive us our trespasses*
> *as we forgive those who trespass*
> *against us,*
> *and lead us not into temptation,*
> *but deliver us from evil.*
> *Amen.*

Second Reading

The leader reads this brief quotation.

Come back to your heart, and from there, to God, for the path is not long from your heart to God. All of the difficulties that are troubling you come from what is outside of you, you who are the exile of your own heart. You let yourself be moved by what is outside of yourself and you lose yourself. You are within, they are outside; gold, silver, and all kinds of money, clothes, clients, the family, they are all outside.

SAINT AUGUSTINE

Prayer for Mercy for the Sick

The leader shares this prayer with those present.

Almighty and everlasting God,
who is the eternal salvation
of those who believe in you,
hear us on behalf of those who are sick,
for whom we beg the help of your mercy.
May their health be restored
if you see that it is good for them,
and may they give you thanks in your Church.
Through Christ our Lord.
　R. Amen.

Let us remember in these prayers all who are sick and in need, our doctors, nurses, and caregivers, all our relatives and friends, living and dead, and the souls of all those recently deceased, as we seek the intercession of the Holy Mother of God, and say together:

R. Hail Mary, full of grace,
the Lord is with thee.
Blessed art thou among women
and blessed is the fruit of thy womb Jesus.
Holy Mary, Mother of God,
pray for us sinners,
now and at the hour of our death.
Amen.

Prayer of Spiritual Communion

Making the sign of the cross, the leader says this prayer.

My Jesus,
I believe you are present
in the Blessed Sacrament.
I love you above all things,
and desire you in my soul.
Since I cannot receive you—
please come spiritually into my heart
as though you are in me
and give to me your healing touch this way.
I unite myself to you,
never allow me to be separated from you.
R. Amen.

The leader concludes by saying to those present:

May the Lord be with you always,
to be your strength and your peace.
    R. *Thanks be to God.*

Appendix

✳

Communion of the Sick
Outside of Mass

The following appendix presents the English translation, original texts, and arrangement of material from the Pastoral Care of the Sick: Rites of Anointing and Viaticum *(copyright 1982, International Committee on English in the Liturgy) and excerpts from the English translation of* Holy Communion and Worship of the Eucharist Outside of Mass *(copyright 1974, ICEL). All rights to this material reside with the International Committee on English in the Liturgy.*

Please note that the Rite for the Distribution of Holy Communion is a freestanding liturgy and should not be incorporated into any devotional service. Thus, when Holy Communion is brought to the sick from the Church, the extraordinary minister must use the ritual found in this appendix. The Rite of Distribution of Holy Communion should not be combined with devotional prayers, even those contained in this book. However, following the Rite for the Distribution of Holy Communion, the prayers in this book may be used as a continuing reflection on the wonderful healing God gives us in the Blessed Sacrament.

Introduction

This appendix contains two rites: one for use when communion can be celebrated in the context of a liturgy of the word; the other, a brief communion rite for use in more restrictive circumstances, such as in hospitals.

Priests with pastoral responsibilities should see to it that the sick or aged, even though not seriously ill or in danger of death, are given every opportunity to receive the eucharist frequently, even daily, especially during the Easter season. They may receive communion at any hour. Those who care for the sick may receive communion with them, in accord with the usual norms. To provide frequent communion for the sick, it may be necessary to ensure that the community has a sufficient number of ministers of communion. The communion minister should wear attire appropriate to this ministry.

The sick person and others may help to plan the celebration, for example, by choosing the prayers and readings. Those making these choices should keep in mind the condition of the sick person. The readings and the homily should help those present to reach a deeper understanding of the mystery of human suffering in relation to the paschal mystery of Christ.

The faithful who are ill are deprived of their rightful and accustomed place in the eucharistic community. In bringing communion to them the minister of communion represents Christ and manifests faith and charity on behalf of the whole community toward those who cannot be present at the eucharist. For the sick the reception of communion is not only a privilege but also a sign of support and concern shown by the Christian community for its members who are ill.

The links between the community's eucharistic celebration, especially on the Lord's Day, and the communion of the sick are intimate and manifold. Besides remembering the sick in the general intercessions at Mass, those present should be reminded occasionally of the significance of communion in the lives of those who are ill: union with Christ in his struggle with evil, his prayer for the world, and his love for the Father, and union with the community from which they are separated.

The obligation to visit and comfort those who cannot take part in the eucharistic assembly may be clearly demonstrated by taking communion to them from the community's eucharistic celebration. This symbol of unity between the community and its sick members has the deepest significance on the Lord's Day, the special day of the eucharistic assembly.

When the eucharist is brought to the sick, it should be carried in a pyx or a small closed container. Those who are with the sick should be asked to prepare a table covered with a linen cloth upon which the blessed sacrament will be placed. Lighted candles are prepared and, where it is customary, a vessel of holy water. Care should be taken to make the occasion special and joyful.

Sick people who are unable to receive communion under the form of bread may receive it under the form of wine alone. If the wine is consecrated at a Mass not celebrated in the presence of the sick person, the blood of the Lord is kept in a properly covered vessel and is placed in the tabernacle after communion. The precious blood should be carried to the sick in a vessel which is closed in such a way as to eliminate all danger of spilling. If some of the precious blood remains, it should be consumed by the minister, who should also see to it that the vessel is properly purified.

If the sick wish to celebrate the sacrament of penance, it is preferable that the priest make himself available for this during a previous visit.

If it is necessary to celebrate the sacrament of penance during the rite of communion, it takes the place of the penitential rite.

Communion in Ordinary Circumstances

If possible, provision should be made to celebrate Mass in the homes of the sick, with their families and friends gathered around them. The Ordinary determines the conditions and requirements for such celebration.

Communion in a Hospital or Institution

There will be situations, particularly in large institutions with many communicants, when the minister should consider alternative means so that the rite of communion of the sick is not diminished to the absolute minimum. In such cases the following alternatives should be considered: (a) where possible, the residents or patients may be gathered in groups in one or more areas; (b) additional ministers of communion may assist.

When it is not possible to celebrate the full rite, the rite for communion in a hospital or institution may be used. If it is convenient, however, the minister may add elements from the rite for ordinary circumstances, for example, a Scripture reading.

The rite begins with the recitation of the eucharistic antiphon in the church, the hospital chapel, or the first room visited. Then the minister gives communion to the sick in their individual rooms.

The concluding prayer may be said in the church, the hospital chapel, or the last room visited. No blessing is given.

Communion of the Sick in Ordinary Circumstances

– Introductory Rites –

Greeting

The minister greets the sick person and the others present. One of the following may be used.

A

The peace of the Lord be with you always.

R. And also with you.

B

Peace be with you (this house) and with all who live here.

R. And also with you.

C

The grace of our Lord Jesus Christ and the love of God and the fellowship of the Holy Spirit be with you all.

R. And also with you.

D

The grace and peace of God our Father and the Lord Jesus Christ be with you.

R. And also with you.

The minister then places the blessed sacrament on the table, and all join in adoration.

Sprinkling With Holy Water

If it seems desirable, the priest or deacon may sprinkle the sick person and those present with holy water. One of the following may be used:

A
Let this water call to mind our baptism into Christ, who by his death and resurrection has redeemed us.

B
Like a stream in parched land,
may the grace of the Lord refresh our lives.

If the sacrament of penance is now celebrated, the penitential rite is omitted. In case of necessity, this may be a generic confession.

Penitential Rite

The minister invites the sick person and all present to join in the penitential rite, using these or similar words:

A
My brothers and sisters, to prepare ourselves for this celebration, let us call to mind our sins.

B
My brothers and sisters, let us turn with confidence to the Lord and ask his forgiveness for all our sins.

After a brief period of silence, the penitential rite continues, using one of the following:

A

Lord Jesus, you healed the sick:
Lord, have mercy.
R. Lord, have mercy.

Lord Jesus, you forgave sinners:
Christ, have mercy.
R. Christ, have mercy.

Lord Jesus, you give us yourself to heal us
     and bring us strength:
Lord, have mercy.
R. Lord, have mercy.

B
All say:

I confess to almighty God,
and to you, my brothers and sisters,
that I have sinned through my own fault
     They strike their breast.
in my thoughts and in my words,
in what I have done,
and in what I have failed to do;
and I ask blessed Mary, ever virgin,
all the angels and saints,
and you, my brothers and sisters,
to pray for me to the Lord our God.

The minister concludes the penitential rite with the following:

May almighty God have mercy on us,
forgive us our sins,
and bring us to everlasting life.
R. *Amen.*

– Liturgy of the Word –

Reading

The word of God is proclaimed by one of those present or by the minister. One of the following readings may be used:

A

A reading from the holy gospel
according to John (6:51)

Jesus says:
"I myself am the living bread
come down from heaven.
If anyone eats this bread
he shall live forever;
the bread I will give
is my flesh, for the life of the world."
    This is the Gospel of the Lord.

B

A reading from the holy gospel
according to John (6:54–58)

Jesus says:
"He who feeds on my flesh
and drinks my blood
has life eternal,
and I will raise him up on the last day.
For my flesh is real food
and my blood real drink.
The man who feeds on my flesh
and drinks my blood
remains in me, and I in him.
Just as the Father who has life sent me
and I have life because of the Father,
so the man who feeds on me
will have life because of me.
This is the bread that came down from heaven.
Unlike your ancestors who ate and died nonetheless,
the man who feeds on this bread shall live forever."
　　This is the Gospel of the Lord.

C

A reading from the holy gospel according to
John (14:6)

Jesus says:
"I am the way, and the truth, and the life;
no one comes to the Father but through me."
　　This is the Gospel of the Lord.

D

A reading from the holy gospel
according to John (15:5)

Jesus says:
"I am the vine, you are the branches.
He who lives in me and I in him,
will produce abundantly,
for apart from me you can do nothing."
This is the Gospel of the Lord.

E

A reading from the first letter of
John (4:16)

We have come to know and to believe
in the love God has for us.
God is love,
and he who abides in love
abides in God,
and God in him.
This is the Word of the Lord.

Response

A brief period of silence may be observed after the reading of the word of God. The minister may then give a brief explanation of the reading, applying it to the needs of the sick person and those who are looking after him or her.

General Intercessions

The general intercessions may be said. With a brief introduction the minister invites all those present to pray. After the intentions the minister says the concluding prayer. It is desirable that the intentions be announced by someone other than the minister.

– Liturgy of Holy Communion –

The Lord's Prayer

The minister introduces the Lord's Prayer in these or similar words:

A

Now let us pray as Christ the Lord has taught us:

B

And now let us pray with confidence as Christ our Lord commanded:

All say:

> Our Father...

Communion

The minister shows the eucharistic bread to those present, saying:

A

This is the bread of life.
Taste and see that the Lord is good.

B

This is the Lamb of God
who takes away the sins of the world.
Happy are those who are called to his supper.

The sick person and all who are to receive communion say:

Lord, I am not worthy to receive you,
but only say the word and I shall be healed.

The minister goes to the sick person, and, showing the blessed sacrament, says:

The body of Christ.

The sick person answers: "Amen," and receives communion.

Then the minister says:

The blood of Christ.

The sick person answers: "Amen," and receives communion. Others present who wish to receive communion then do so in the usual way.

After the conclusion of the rite, the minister cleanses the vessel as usual.

Silent Prayer

Then a period of silence may be observed.

Prayer After Communion

The minister says a concluding prayer. One of the following may be used:

Let us pray.

Pause for silent prayer, if this has not preceded.

A
God our Father,
you have called us to share the one bread
and one cup
and so become one in Christ.

Help us to live in him
that we may bear fruit,
rejoicing that he has redeemed the world.

We ask this through Christ our Lord.
R. Amen.

B
All-powerful God,
we thank you for the nourishment you give us
through your holy gift.

Pour out your Spirit upon us
and in the strength of this food from heaven
keep us single-minded in your service.

We ask this in the name of Jesus the Lord.
R. Amen.

– Concluding Rite –

Blessing

The priest or deacon blesses the sick person and the others present, using one of the following blessings. If, however, any of the blessed sacrament remains, he may bless the sick person by making a sign of the cross with the blessed sacrament, in silence.

A

May God the Father bless you.
R. Amen.
May God the Son heal you.
R. Amen.
May God the Holy Spirit enlighten you.
R. Amen.
May almighty God bless you,
the Father, and the Son, and the Holy Spirit.
R. Amen.

B

May the Lord be with you to protect you.
R. Amen.
May he guide you and give you strength.
R. Amen.

May he watch over you, keep you in his care,
and bless you with his peace.
R. *Amen.*
May almighty God bless you,
the Father, and the Son, and the Holy Spirit.
R. *Amen.*

C
May the blessing of almighty God,
the Father, and the Son, and the Holy Spirit,
come upon you and remain with you for ever.
R. *Amen.*

A minister who is not a priest or deacon invokes God's blessing and makes the sign of the cross on himself or herself, while saying:

A
May the Lord bless us,
protect us from all evil,
and bring us to everlasting life.
R. *Amen.*

B
May the almighty and merciful God bless
    and protect us,
the Father, and the Son, and the Holy Spirit.
R. *Amen.*

✳

Communion in a
Hospital or Institution

– Introductory Rite –

Antiphon

*The rite may begin in the church, the hospital chapel, or
the first room, where the minister says one of the following antiphons:*

A
How holy this feast
in which Christ is our food:
his passion is recalled;
grace fills our hearts;
and we receive a pledge of the glory to come.

B
How gracious you are, Lord:
your gift of bread from heaven
reveals a Father's love and brings us perfect joy.
You fill the hungry with good things
and send the rich away empty.

C
I am the living bread
come down from heaven.

If you eat this bread
you will live for ever.
The bread I will give is my flesh
for the life of the world.

*If it is customary, the minister may be accompanied by a
person carrying a candle.*

– Liturgy of Holy Communion –

Greeting

*On entering each room, the minister may use one of the
following greetings:*

A
The peace of the Lord be with you always.
R. *And also with you.*

B
**The grace of our Lord Jesus Christ and the love of
God and the fellowship of the Holy Spirit be with
you all.**
R. *And also with you.*

*The minister then places the blessed sacrament on the
table, and all join in adoration.*

*If there is time and it seems desirable, the minister may
proclaim a Scripture reading from those found on pages
275–277.*

The Lord's Prayer

When circumstances permit (for example, when there are not many rooms to visit), the minister is encouraged to lead the sick in the Lord's Prayer. The minister introduces the Lord's Prayer in these or similar words:

A

Jesus taught us to call God our Father, and so we have the courage to say:

B

Now let us pray as Christ the Lord has taught us:

All say:

Our Father…

Communion

The minister shows the eucharistic bread to those present, saying:

A

This is the Lamb of God
who takes away the sins of the world.
Happy are those who hunger and thirst,
for they shall be satisfied.

B

This is the bread of life.
Taste and see that the Lord is good.

The sick person and all who are to receive communion say:

Lord, I am not worthy to receive you,
but only say the word and I shall be healed.

The minister goes to the sick person and, showing the blessed sacrament, says:

The body of Christ.

The sick person answers: "Amen," and receives communion.

Then the minister says:

The blood of Christ

The sick person answers: "Amen," and receives communion. Others present who wish to receive communion then do so in the usual way.

– Concluding Rite –

Concluding Prayer
The concluding prayer may be said either in the last room visited, in the church, or chapel. One of the following may be used.

Let us pray.
Pause for silent prayer.

A
God our Father,

you have called us to share the one bread
and one cup
and so become one in Christ.

Help us to live in him
that we may bear fruit,
rejoicing that he has redeemed the world.

We ask this through Christ our Lord.
R. *Amen.*

B
All-powerful and ever-living God,
may the body and blood of Christ your Son
be for our brothers and sisters
a lasting remedy for body and soul.

We ask this through Christ our Lord.
R. *Amen.*

C
All-powerful God,
we thank you for the nourishment you give us
through your holy gift.

Pour out your Spirit upon us
and in the strength of this food from heaven
keep us single-minded in your service.

We ask this in the name of Jesus the Lord.
R. *Amen.*

The blessing is omitted and the minister cleanses the vessel as usual.

Movable Dates for Observances of the Church Year

YEARS	2003	2004	2005	2006	2007
First Sunday of Advent	Nov. 30	Nov. 28	Nov. 27	Dec. 3	Dec. 2
Weeks of Ordinary Time Before Lent	8	7	5	8	7
Baptism of Our Lord	Jan. 12	Jan. 11	Jan. 9	Jan. 8	Jan. 7
Ash Wednesday	Mar. 5	Feb. 25	Feb. 9	Mar. 1	Feb. 21
Easter Sunday	Apr. 20	Apr. 11	Mar. 27	Apr. 16	Apr. 8
Ascension of Our Lord	May 29	May 20	May 5	May 25	May 17
Pentecost	June 8	May 30	May 15	June 4	May 27
Week of Ordinary Time Resumed After Pentecost	10	9	7	9	8
Holy Trinity	June 15	June 6	May 22	June 11	June 3
Corpus Christi	June 22	June 13	May 29	June 18	June 10

YEARS	2008	2009	2010	2011	2012
First Sunday of Advent	Nov. 30	Nov. 29	Nov. 28	Nov. 27	Dec. 2
Weeks of Ordinary Time Before Lent	4	7	6	9	7
Baptism of Our Lord	Jan. 13	Jan. 11	Jan. 10	Jan. 9	Jan. 8
Ash Wednesday	Feb. 6	Feb. 25	Feb. 17	Mar. 9	Feb. 22
Easter Sunday	Mar. 23	Apr. 12	Apr. 4	Apr. 24	Apr. 8
Ascension of Our Lord	May 1	May 21	May 13	June 2	May 17
Pentecost	May 11	May 31	May 23	June 12	May 27
Week of Ordinary Time Resumed After Pentecost	6	9	8	11	8
Holy Trinity	May 18	June 7	May 30	June 19	June 3
Corpus Christi	May 25	June 14	June 6	June 26	June 10

Index to Prayers

A

Acceptance 217
Act of Worship 42
Affliction 73
All Saints 213
All Souls 218, 221
Annunciation 70
Anxiety 63
Ascension 149, 152
Ash Wednesday 76
Assumption 185

B

Beatitudes 214
Before Surgery 62
Belief 173
Blind 244

C

Candle Prayers xix
Change 20
Charity 167
Christian Unity 48, 52
Comfort 62, 210, 252
Communion, spiritual 264
Communion (unable to
    receive) 143

Compassion 20
Courage 40
Cross, Contemplation of
    110, 128
Cure for Suffering 17

D

Disabled 183, 260
Discouragement 142

E

Emotional Healing 243
Eucharist 233
Evening Prayer 190
Example, Good 127, 199

F

Faith 57, 95, 123
Faithfulness 90
Family 32, 56
Fear 172
Forgiveness 105
Francis of Assisi 196, 199, 200

G

God's Care 211, 239
God of Love 31
Guidance 147

H

Healing 12, 21, 132, 162, 239, 243
Healing–help 138, 253
Health 259
Heaven, treasures of 122
Holy Communion (unable to receive) 143
Holy Spirit 47, 50, 157, 158

I

Illness 194
Isolation 237

J

Joseph, Saint 64
Joy 26
Justice 205

L

Life 46, 117
Loneliness 74
Lost Souls 99
Lourdes 248
Love 42, 137

M

Magnificat 186
Mercy for the Sick 263
Missionaries 204
Mission Sunday 201
Morning 40

N

Need(s) 11
Newman, John Henry 195
Night 248

O

Our Lady 36, 188, 247

P

Pain 177, 178
Patience 216
Peace 94, 195

R

Reassurance 222
Renewal 95, 153, 168
Repentance 79
Request 89
Resurrection 116

S

Salvation 85
Serenity 80
Seriously ill 255, 258
Service to Humankind (Vocations) 133
Sickness, for help in 182, 232
Souls, Lost 99
Strength 84, 104, 163
Suffering(s) 6, 7, 37, 222
Suffering, Curable 17
Support 148
Surgery, Before 62

T

Tension and Change 20
Thanksgiving 225, 227, 233
Transfiguration 179
Trust in God 217, 232

U

Unable to Receive
  Communion 143
Understanding 112
Unity, Christian 52
Unselfishness 16

V

Vocations 133

W

Weary 104
Wisdom 100
World Mission Sunday 201
Worry 67, 68
Worship 42

Sources and Acknowledgments

✠

The compiler wishes to express his gratitude to the following who granted permission to reproduce or adapt material of which they are the authors, publishers, or copyright holders.

The English translation, original texts, arrangement of material from the *Pastoral Care of the Sick: Rites of Anointing and Viaticum* © 1982, International Committee on English in the Liturgy, Inc. (ICEL); excerpts from the English translation of *Holy Communion and Worship of the Eucharist Outside of Mass* © 1974 (ICEL) are used with permission. All rights to this material reside with the International Committee on English in the Liturgy. All rights reserved.

Biblical excerpts from the Scriptures, with the exception of the Psalms, and except where otherwise noted, are from *The Jerusalem Bible*, Popular Edition, Darton, Longman, & Todd, and Doubleday & Co. Used by permission. Excerpts from the Psalms are from the *Christian Community Bible* published by Liguori Publications, Liguori, Missouri. All rights reserved.

Other permissions are as follows:

"Act of Worship," p. 42, from a mission given at St. Joseph's, Bromley, 1998. Used with permission.